# COWBOYS ESSENTIAL

Everything You Need to Know
to Be a Real Fan!

Frank Luksa

T0163174

TRIUMPH
B O O K S
CHICAGO

Library of Congress Cataloging-in-Publication Data

Luksa, Frank.
   Cowboys essential : everything you need to know to be a real fan / Frank Luksa.
    p. cm.
   ISBN-13: 978-1-57243-861-3
   ISBN-10: 1-57243-861-4
   1. Dallas Cowboys (Football team)—History. 2. Dallas Cowboys (Football team)—Miscellanea. I. Title.

GV956.D3L84 2006
796.332'64097642812—dc22

2006009684

This book is available in quantity at special discounts for your group or organization. For further information, contact:

**Triumph Books**
542 South Dearborn Street
Suite 750
Chicago, Illinois 60605
(312) 939-3330
Fax (312) 663-3557

Printed in U.S.A.
ISBN-13: 978-1-57243-861-3
ISBN-10: 1-57243-861-4
Design by Patricia Frey
All photos courtesy of AP/Wide World Photos except where otherwise indicated

# Contents

# Foreword

*Cowboys Essential* is the history of the Dallas Cowboys from a unique viewpoint that will appeal to all fans. The title of the book is perfect. It's essential reading for anyone who wants to know more about the Cowboys or thinks he knows everything about them already.

Anyone who has followed the Cowboys is aware of the outline of franchise history. How a nearly winless 1960 expansion team rose to win Super Bowls and more games than any NFL team during the '70s. How it fell and rose again to dominate the 1990s by winning three more Super Bowls.

The *Cowboys Essential* approach is different from reviews devoted too often to dull play-by-play. All key games are here, from Super Bowl to Ice Bowl and Hail Mary, to be sure. But the emphasis is on what those involved said and thought. That's what makes this book different. It's about people.

It unfolds as personal anecdotes from players, coaches, and opponents that range from high humor to lowbrow drama. There's as much fun as facts in these pages.

Trivia adds to the appeal of *Cowboys Essential.* One question in particular stumped me. It asks which Cowboy holds the record for appearing in the most playoff games. I got it wrong. See if you do better.

You'll also see top-10 rankings by position and a few fascinating quotes. In the latter category, I recommend Pete Gent's definition of *paranoid* and Eddie LeBaron's description of players on the 1960 expansion roster.

Come to think of it, I recommend everything in *Cowboys Essential.*

—Roger Staubach

# In the Beginning

A story old enough to grow Spanish moss persists, which claims that Clint Murchison Jr. obtained the National Football League expansion franchise in Dallas for a song, but that's not entirely true. It's only partially true.

The musical saga did allow Murchison to enter the NFL one year sooner than some owners at first were willing to approve. Had he been delayed even 12 months, the history of the Cowboys would have been altered to perhaps a less fruitful and fascinating evolution.

The song became a swing factor after the NFL owners meeting in Miami in January of 1960 where they finally selected a new commissioner. That decision took them seven days and 22 ballots before settling on a compromise candidate. He was 33-year-old Pete Rozelle, an ironic choice for Tex Schramm, general manager of Murchison's team-to-be, who as GM of the Los Angeles Rams eight years earlier hired Rozelle as his publicity director.

Expansion was the next topic, and opinion also split on that issue. A faction led by Chicago's George Halas favored hustling a team into existence to compete against Lamar Hunt's just-hatched American Football League, set to debut that summer in Dallas. George Preston Marshall of Washington led a group entrenched in expansion delay. Another impasse loomed.

Marshall was a pioneer of elaborate pregame and halftime shows, which were often more entertaining than his teams. Pride in his band and pom-pom girls ran deep. However, years earlier Marshall had dismissed band director Barney Briskin, composer of the fight song, "Hail to the Redskins."

Briskin contacted attorney Tom Webb, Murchison's representative in Washington, explained that he and Marshall had split, and offered Webb

**DID YOU KNOW . . .** That the first player to touch the ball in a regular season Cowboys game was Tom Franckhauser, a defensive back and kick returner?

the rights to the song. Webb accepted, figuring it was useful for a joke on Marshall. When Marshall learned that Murchison, through Webb, owned his fight song, he belched smoke.

So a deal was done. If Webb returned the song rights to Marshall, the Redskins owner would vote for immediate expansion into Dallas. Webb agreed. The transfer was put in writing, Marshall upheld his part of the bargain, and thus Murchison became an NFL owner.

Murchison paid $600,000 for the privilege. Of that total, $50,000 accounted for the franchise fee and over time became worth multiple millions. The remaining $550,000 went for the right to draft 36 players from 12 established clubs, all of whom made certain none of them was worth keeping. Neither were most of the players worth having, as they confirmed to the Cowboys during a 0–11–1 maiden season.

Murchison became a model owner, loyal and patient above all, composed in real or imagined crisis. He was among the last of his kind—the sportsman/owner whose financial health lay aside from pro football profit. His mega-millions were spread so wide and far and invested in so many venues that Murchison once asked for reservations in a hotel that he'd forgotten he owned.

The public never appreciated Murchison's understated leadership as the foundation of future success. He hired Tom Landry and Schramm, who in turn hired Gil Brandt as head scout, and left them alone. He never interfered with their decisions or objected to any expense—from flying a team to California for training camp or introducing computer-driven evaluations to the scouting process.

Murchison was asked if he ever ordered Landry to call a play for him. His droll humor surfaced.

"I do not offer suggestions to Tom Landry," he said. "Furthermore, Landry never makes any suggestions as to how I conduct my sixth-grade football team, which incidentally is undefeated. We have a professional standoff."

Murchison cut a slight 5'9" figure topped by an inch-high crew cut and thick-lens glasses. He was shy in public, a confirmed gagster with a rapier wit in private. He was also a brilliant man who earned a master's degree from the Massachusetts Institute of Technology, where he played a spot of underweight halfback. *The Miami Herald* columnist Edwin Pope once used that gridiron nugget in a piece that referred to Murchison as "a 130-pound former halfback at MIT."

A classic Clint letter followed that read:

> *Dear Ed:*
> *With reference to your recent column about the Dallas Cowboys, you're full of s\*\*t. I weigh 142 pounds.*

Murchison was a habitual letter writer, and many demonstrated his dust-dry humor during hard times. For example, the attendance drought that plagued the Cowboys during their start-up seasons served as a theme for a 1962 letter to Toots Shor. The New York restaurant owner had obtained four extra box seats for Clint's group for a game against the Giants at Yankee Stadium. To repay Shor for when the Giants played in the Cotton Bowl later that year, Clint shipped a large carton to Toots with this message:

> *Enclosed are the box seats for the New York–Dallas game Sunday about which I spoke to you Friday night. In case you want to bring any of your friends with you, I am also sending you Section 1, 2, 3, and 4.*

Shor opened the carton and found 10,000 unsold tickets.

Murchison's enduring strength lay in his ability to defuse a potentially explosive issue with a deft decision or wickedly pointed remark. These qualities remain ignored or undervalued in many retrospects of franchise history. The courage of his convictions in the men he hired and the course they set never wavered. They in turn fed off his confidence.

An early glimpse of Murchison's vision was seen following the 1963 season when many wanted to be rid of Landry, who had one season left on his five-year contract. Landry's teams had won an unremarkable 13 games in four seasons. Local heat was intense enough that Schramm called Murchison for

## TRIVIA

**Who scored the winning points when the Cowboys won their first NFL game?**

*Answers to the trivia questions are on pages 163–164.*

counsel and advice. Clint chilled the rebellion in February of 1964 with an in-your-face volley to Landry's critics.

He told Schramm to sign Landry to a 10-year contract, an unheard of length of tenure in the NFL or any pro-sports entity. The deal didn't absolve Landry from criticism but it reduced anti-Tom bellows to immaterial noise. Nor was Murchison immune from gentle chiding for what he'd done.

"We lost several games in 1964 after we had given Tom the contract," he recalled. "And after we had lost real bad—really been pummeled to death—I had lunch with a friend, and he said there's a silver lining in all this. He said, 'At least Tom's got only nine years left.'"

More than a decade of ownership passed before Murchison's faith was fully repaid with victory in Super Bowl VI. The 1971 Cowboys beat Miami, 24–3, to ease the stigma of five consecutive playoff failures low-lighted by

*The Cowboys moved into Texas Stadium [shown here in 1996], in 1971. They've won 70 percent of their games in Texas Stadium.*

a goal-line fumble and late interception that donated Super Bowl V to Baltimore, 16–13.

Murchison was sought for reaction to winning the big one that the Cowboys had pursued since 1960. Amidst a wild locker-room celebration, his wry summation went thusly:

## TRIVIA

**Name the ball boy of the '60s who later played for the Cowboys.**

*Answers to the trivia questions are on pages 163–164.*

"This is the successful conclusion of our 12-year plan."

That '71 team also baptized Texas Stadium, the unique, luxury-suites, hole-in-the-roof home of the Cowboys in suburban Irving. Murchison's desire had been to locate it in downtown Dallas, but Mayor J. Eric Jonsson displayed little interest or cooperation in the project. Clint shrugged and built beyond city limits.

The early '70s also brought strain via formation of the World Football League, whose early strategy involved raiding NFL rosters for premier players. Tailback Calvin Hill left the Cowboys for Hawaii. There were rumors that Pro Bowl offensive tackle Rayfield Wright, defensive tackle Jethro Pugh, linebacker D. D. Lewis, and who knew who else might defect. This was not a false alarm, and it demanded the Cowboys' owner address an alarming situation.

So he did, with calm understatement. Asked if he ever thought of counterraiding the WFL to sign its players, Murchison's puckish spirit rose above the occasion.

"If the WFL succeeds," he said, "I don't want to sign their players. I want to sign their accountants."

Murchison would enjoy one more Super Bowl victory and endure two Super Bowl defeats to Pittsburgh as the '70s closed. His ownership had little time left by then. Declining health leading to his death in 1987 forced the sale of the Cowboys in '84 to a group headed by Dallas businessman H. R. (Bum) Bright. The music faded during Bright's brief stewardship.

Hence founder Clint Murchison Jr. departed from the NFL scene, and it is regrettable that few recognize the value of his quiet, confident ownership. When the ragged, formative years of the Cowboys are linked with their ascent to two-time world champion, the pivotal figure emerges. He weighed only 142 pounds.

# Dallas Versus Dallas

During the summer of 1960, one too many professional football teams located in Dallas. Two was an obvious crowd in a city where the sport already had flopped once.

The short-lived Dallas Texans opened the 1952 season in the Cotton Bowl, lost four echo-filled games there, returned the franchise to the league, trained thereafter in Hershey, Pennsylvania, and played the last half of the schedule as a road team. No one dreamed that a big-time future winner left town. But so it was when the franchise transferred to Baltimore in '53 and became the two-time NFL champion Colts in 1958–1959.

Then came the NFL expansion Rangers, who a few weeks into existence changed their nickname to the Cowboys. A lockstep arrival saw another franchise on the scene, the fledgling Dallas Texans of the newly formed American Football League. The duel for survival was spicy because it pitted local millionaires against one another: 37-year-old Clint Murchison Jr. of the Cowboys and AFL founder Lamar Hunt, 28.

Neither would run out of money. But one eventually had to be run out of town. But who, and how long would it take?

The rivals adopted different approaches to attract fans. The Cowboys were staid and conventional, betting on stars from visiting teams to draw customers. The Texans were promotion-prone and cheeky toward the button-down Cowboys. As early as '61 they challenged their NFL neighbor to an exhibition game for charity because, "the public demands it."

This was news to columnist Blackie Sherrod, who wrote, "Dear hearts, the way the 'public' turned out for both the Texan and Cowboy games this year, it could ill afford to demand anything, even mustard for the hot dogs."

Sherrod had the situation pegged. Attendance figures were suspicious, often inflated by generous in-house estimates (Cowboys) or free admissions (Texans) in the absence of accurate turnstile counts until '62. Good seats were always available as the teams rotated Sunday home games in the 75,000-capacity Cotton Bowl. Both franchises oozed red ink.

On a foul Sunday in November of '60 it appeared from the press box that the Cowboys and San Francisco played before an empty stadium. No one was seated in the opposite stands. The few who turned out huddled out of sight below the upper deck on the press box side. Even by a bloated estimate of 10,000—a later confession admitted maybe 3,800 seats were filled—it set an all-time attendance low.

Players recognized that lack of allegiance to either team was so divided that people ignored both. Appearing before a Cowboy Club audience, quarterback Eddie LeBaron referred to scant attendance with an apology for the brevity of his remarks.

"I have to hurry to catch a plane to Amarillo," he said. "A man up there wants to buy two season tickets."

Neither were the Cowboys a hot ticket on the road. On a rainy Sunday in Washington the Redskins beat them, 26–14, although owner George Preston Marshall felt winless Dallas got even by killing his home crowd.

"Too bad we had this rain," said Marshall. "Dallas made $42 above the guarantee ($30,000)."

The Cowboys-Texans rivalry mirrored the larger struggle between the NFL and AFL, which filed and lost an antitrust suit against the established league. The rivals competed to sign college prospects, ignored, insulted, or sued each other for players and in Dallas continued to lose huge amounts of money.

Well into the stalemate Murchison proposed a mock settlement with Hunt.

**DID YOU KNOW . . .** That when asked who would be the winner of the Cowboys-Texan duel for supremacy in Dallas, Houston Oiler scout John Breen cracked, "The first one that leaves town"?

*The Cowboys stumbled in their first few years, losing many lopsided games, such as this 48–7 loss to the Browns in their maiden season. Tom Franckhauser (32) takes down Cleveland's Jim Brown.*

"We'll flip a coin," he said. "The winner gets to leave town."

It was suggested to billionaire oilman H. L. Hunt that he must be worried about son Lamar's pro football losses, which surely amounted to $1 million a year.

"Oh, I am, I am," replied the elder Hunt. "At that rate he will be broke in 200 years."

So it went for the first season. The Cowboys finished 0–11–1, and drew that phantom 10,000 for its final home game. The Texans went 8–6 and claimed 18,000 attended its home swan song against Buffalo. Two years later the Texans closed with an 11–3 record and won the AFL West title. Yet fewer than 20,000 watched their final two Cotton Bowl games. The Cowboys attracted crowds of 12,692 and 24,226 over the same homestretch.

Brave talk aside, their duel had reached an end in 1962.

"Two teams can't thrive here," Hunt said. "We're planning on the Texans being here and in operation. I can't speak for the other side."

Murchison spoke grimly in response: "As long as the Texans are here, there will be two teams."

By now both had assembled a nucleus of solid to elite talent: Hall of Fame–bound Bob Lilly, Don Perkins, Don Meredith, George Andrie, Frank Clarke, Mike Connelly, Chuck Howley, and Jerry Tubbs were among those of the Cowboys. The Texans' featured players included future HOF quarterback Len Dawson, Jim Tyrer, Jerry Mays, Johnny Robinson, E. J. Holub, and Fred Arbanas.

The latter group made its swan song to Dallas in Houston by winning the AFL championship over the Oilers in the longest game played to that point—sudden-death overtime that lasted 77 minutes, 54 seconds. The Texans overcame a colossal brain lock by captain Abner Haynes who won the OT coin flip only to lose the first offensive possession and wind advantage by blurting, "We'll kick to the clock." The Texans prevailed anyway, 20–17.

The duel in Dallas ended when Hunt moved his franchise to Kansas City for the 1963 season. For the second time within the space of a decade, a future world champion left Dallas. The Chiefs twice beat the Cowboys to the pinnacle event—losing Super Bowl I to Green Bay and winning Super Bowl IV over Minnesota. The difference was that another future world champion remained in Dallas and, over time, competed in more Super Bowls (eight) and won as many (five) as any NFL team.

The Cowboys at last had Dallas to themselves. Dallas reacted with mild curiosity as the 1963 season opened.

## TRIVIA

**Where did the Cowboys hold their first training camp?**

*Answers to the trivia questions are on pages 163–164.*

# Will They Ever Get It Right?

As early as 1963 the Cowboys developed a persona that would attach like a barnacle and stick with them for the next 40-odd years. Columnist Sam Blair best described their exasperating character.

"Excitement, suspense, shock, bewilderment, delight, disgust. The Cowboys caused them at one time or another, occasionally all in the same game. There wasn't a team more glamorous or galling," Blair wrote.

The seasons of '61 through '64 were the wilderness years for Tom Landry, whose teams appeared trapped in a squirrel cage that rotated but went nowhere. Progress was incremental, if not invisible, as near identical returns of 4–9–1, 5–8–1, 4–10, and 5–8–1 followed in numbing sequence.

Landry projected that the Cowboys would be a contender in five years. His five-year plan was five years old, they weren't contenders, and there were few signs that they would be any time soon. Landry later confessed that this period was the worst of his 29-year coaching career in Dallas.

"The first three seasons didn't bother me a great deal," he reminisced. "I was just trying to make us interesting to watch, biding time until we had enough boys to play. I wavered some in '63, when we really weren't producing as I felt we should, and then it continued in '64. It was a real low year for me."

What confounded Landry, frazzled fans, and dejected players was the rich and varied ways the Cowboys found to lose. Young and erratic quarterback Don Meredith, untrained to read defenses as an SMU star, drew most of the blame to the rancorous point that he was booed during pregame introductions. Landry stood second as a bust, his reputation as a football genius a hollow accolade. It was openly questioned whether he could coach foam to rise.

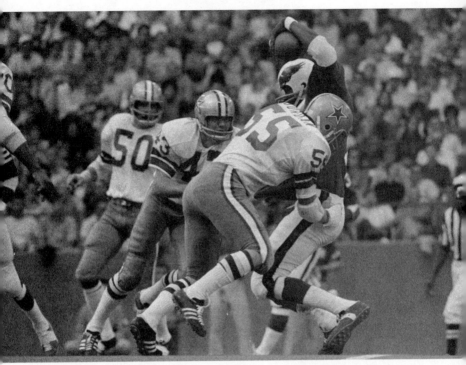

*Future Hall of Famer Lee Roy Jordan, here in action against the Eagles in 1971, was drafted by the Cowboys in 1963 and became a fixture on the defense that was the strength of the team through the early years*

Worse, a prophet far ahead of his time and himself muddled the scene by predicting unreasonable outcomes. Tex Maule, pro football guru for *Sports Illustrated,* made the Cowboys his choice in '63 to win the Eastern Division. Maule reasoned that Landry's high-tech offense of shifts, motion, and reverses that averaged 28 points per game the year before would return. He forgot that Landry's unique flex defense remained immature, Meredith unpredictable, and the players unacquainted with playoff pressure.

More predictably, the Cowboys were often the epitome of football folly. They lost in '62 to Chicago, 34–33, by the margin of the game's most automatic play—a blocked extra point. That hadn't happened to them since '60 when they lost to Philadelphia (27–25) via *two* blocked extra points.

They lost in San Francisco 31–24 in '63 on the day Meredith set a still-standing club record of 460 passing yards in a single game. The outcome was influenced when cornerback Cornell Green was ejected for kicking at an opponent even though, in keeping with Cowboys accuracy, he missed his target. Fullback Amos Marsh also fumbled a perfect pitchout and created a turnover the 49ers used to launch their winning touchdown.

An acid review in the local press summarized how those events affected the final score. It read: "Two things happened [that] contributed heavily to the misfortune: Cornell Green got thrown out of the game and Amos Marsh didn't."

To infuriate fans and strain allegiance further, the Cowboys habitually saved humiliating pratfalls for their largest home crowds. They did it for five consecutive years through '64. For instance, roughly double the usual audience (an estimated 41,500) turned out in '61 for the New York Giants kickoff.

The Cowboys played the then-powerful Giants tight into the third quarter when the usual disaster occurred. Erich Barnes returned an Eddie LeBaron pass an NFL-record 102 yards to turn the game into a 31–10 rout. That was bad enough, but films showed that as Barnes ran past the Cowboys' bench, Meredith and Jerry Tubbs each extended his right foot to trip the opponent. Again, true to the Cowboys' embryonic form, they missed Barnes.

When Meredith didn't foul up by overthrowing a touchdown he could have made by running, his offensive line imploded. Of course, most offensive lines did when overrun by the Fearsome Foursome of the Los Angeles Rams—Lamar Lundy, Roosevelt Grier, Merlin Olsen, and Deacon Jones. They treated Meredith like a piñata, sacking the Dallas passer seven times during an exhibition in '64.

"Seven times is bad but lurking behind that statistic is something horrible," went *The Dallas Morning News* report. "It is to Meredith's credit that he ever got rid of the ball at all, and a half dozen times he threw from a position better suited to being embalmed."

The Dallas *Times Herald* man wrote, "A new statistic was invented for the game—yards lost attempting to live."

## TRIVIA

Who said this about the Cowboys in the early '60s?: "There were a lot of old-timers. We had 27 knees to be taped every day in practice; in several cases two on one player. We had old age, bad knees, and sometimes bad attitude."

*Answers to the trivia questions are on pages 163–164.*

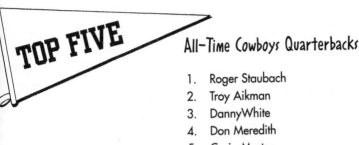

**TOP FIVE**

### All-Time Cowboys Quarterbacks

1. Roger Staubach
2. Troy Aikman
3. Danny White
4. Don Meredith
5. Craig Morton

Yet it was during a '62 Cowboys-Pittsburgh game in the Cotton Bowl that the all-time weird sequence unfolded. Only those loopy Cowboys could produce a play so bizarre that no living witness had ever seen it before. That was to turn *their* NFL record-length touchdown pass into two points for the Steelers.

The sequence began from the Dallas 1-yard line when LeBaron connected deep with Frank Clarke, who completed an apparent 99-yard touchdown and the longest scoring pass in NFL history. This put LeBaron into select company with himself since a year earlier he completed the shortest-ever touchdown pass to Dick Bielksi from a distance of two inches.

The Cowboys celebrated tying the game at 21–all, but not for long. A red penalty flag lay at the Dallas goal line. An official saw guard Andy Cvercko holding all 280 pounds of Big Daddy Lipscomb, Pittsburgh's defensive tackle. Referee Emil Heintz confirmed that the infraction occurred two yards deep in the end zone. Therefore, according to a rule known only to Heintz, and certainly not to Landry, who for the only time in his career marched to midfield in protesting disbelief, the Steelers were awarded a safety.

The natural order of things followed. The Cowboys lost by the margin of that safety, 30–28.

Somewhere during this period the first known wisecrack by stoic Landry was recorded. During the season that the Cowboys switched to a jet engine plane for their team charters, the team hit a rut of two losses and a tie. Landry was asked if he could think of any changes that might help.

"Well," he sighed, "we could go back to a DC-7."

# The Man in the Funny Hat

Tom Landry's personality remained a puzzle as the 1965 season opened. The most generous observation was that he didn't have one.

Reserved by nature, stoic in the arena by training, and distant from players by professional necessity, Landry's rigid composure left everyone wondering what manner of man was concealed behind the mask. Or whether anything other than wires and circuits laid within this taciturn Texan from Mission in the Rio Grande Valley.

Players had complained about Landry's strict, aloof approach since the expansion season in 1960. Tom Franckhauser, one of the original Cowboys, described Landry as thoroughly unpopular with his troops.

"Everyone, including me, uttered discontent," he said. "But I imagine everyone was mad at George Washington at Valley Forge, too."

Many who observed Landry's entire tenure with the Cowboys thought Walt Garrison got it right. Someone asked the retired fullback if he'd ever seen Landry smile. Garrison's reply added to the perception of Landry as robotic.

"No," said Garrison, "but I only played for him [for] nine years."

Landry's mad scientist football schemes clashed with this accepted persona. He invented a unique Flex Defense based on gap-control theory. Bob Lilly said that by the time a player fully understood Landry's creation it was time to retire.

"Tom Landry is a perfectionist," Don Meredith confirmed. "If he was married to Raquel Welch, he'd expect her to cook."

Perfection extended to Landry's impeccable wardrobe. He wore exquisitely tailored suits, a tie to match, and a trademark hat. Former New York

Giants teammate and Cowboys assistant Dick Nolan pointed to Landry's wife Alicia as the fashion expert who dictated her husband's stylish appearance.

"If Alicia didn't dress Tom, he'd still be wearing bib overalls from Mission," Nolan joked.

The offense Landry designed was one-of-a-kind. It contained a myriad mix of shifts, men in motion, and shell game plays such as double screens, flea flickers, screen passes, and reverses. He aimed to confuse the defense, concealing the actual intent of the attack. What separated Landry from others with variations of these exotic plays was confidence and nerve to risk using them.

Landry's playbook, its intricate patterns seemingly borrowed from sketches on an Egyptian tomb, became an object of amusement. New York Giants publicist Don Smith joked that the playbook wound up in a Chinese laundry, which returned three shirts and a pillowcase. Pete Gent's morbid advice received wide circulation when he told a rookie: "Don't bother reading it, kid. Everyone dies in the end."

The breadth of Landry's 29-year Cowboys career has been well documented. He ranks third all-time behind Don Shula and George Halas with 270 victories. His teams won two Super Bowls, lost three by a combined margin of 11 points, and set an NFL record with 20 consecutive winning seasons. The Pro Football Hall of Fame inducted him as a member in 1990.

Other personal facts about Landry have faded with time, especially those that challenge his reflection as one-dimensional. True, he wasn't prone to small talk. His priorities in life were God, family, and football in that order. He hailed from a generation that endured the Depression and survived combat during WWII.

Landry flew 30 Air Force missions from London over Europe at age 20. One mission crash-landed in France and stripped both wings from his B-17 bomber before it came to rest with the nose nudging a huge tree trunk. In another, engines fizzled when a fuel transfer failed. Landry gave the order to bail out. Seconds before the crew jumped, he jiggled a switch

# TRIVIA

**Which long-time American League football coach was considered for the Cowboys' first head coach position?**

*Answers to the trivia questions are on pages 163–164.*

that brought the engines back to life. That act prevented parachuting into German-occupied Belgium and probable fate as a POW.

Landry's self-control was legendary and illustrated during a game against the Los Angeles Rams. He suddenly left the Anaheim Stadium field surrounded by a police escort. He returned shortly and, as later revealed, wore a bulletproof vest under his coat to protect against a death threat.

Danny White, injured and signaling plays to the quarterback, recalled how Landry reacted to a potential sniper in the stands. "As serious as he could be, he said, 'You better not stand too close because they might miss me and hit you.' I've thought about it over the years and wondered how many other coaches would have come back on the field."

But there were times when emotion got the better of Landry and his self-control broke. He shed postgame tears in a Pittsburgh locker room and told players he'd failed them when the Cowboys hit a 2–5 bottom in 1965. Nor could he finish his farewell address to players after being fired in 1989. The man in the funny hat, as the retiring Roger Staubach called him, was vulnerable to emotion after all.

Roster cut-downs affected him when they included players he privately favored. One such casualty was try-hard linebacker Ken Hutcherson, who carried a Bible with his playbook. When the 1975 draft landed a projected all-linebacker cast of Randy White, Thomas Henderson, and Bob Breunig, Hutcherson had to go.

White, Henderson, and Breunig were standing together in a Valley Ranch hallway when Landry, fresh from cutting Hutcherson, strode past. He swept on without breaking stride and with a sad face he told the intimidated rookies, "I hope you're worth it."

The years are littered with instances of kind, generous gestures Landry made to players and camp followers. He avoided calling attention to them, as in the case of Drew Pearson, hospitalized after a car accident that killed his brother. Pearson recalled that every time orderlies turned him from one side of the bed to the other, the first

## TRIVIA

Who said, "My daddy said, 'If they don't want you or you're not good enough, come back home. But if you quit because you're not tough enough, just keep on going north.'?"

*Answers to the trivia questions are on pages 163–164.*

*The eternally composed Tom Landry watches the Cowboys clinch the division title in a game against the Eagles on December 13, 1981.*

That Tom Landry's teams were shut out only two times in 29 years, 38–0 against St. Louis in 1970 and 44–0 against Chicago in 1985?

face he saw was Landry's. A beat writer recuperating from a heart attack received a get-well phone call from the coach.

Landry demonstrated patience with mavericks and rebels. He strained to understand Duane Thomas, who spent the 1971 season mute over a contract dispute, and Thomas Henderson, whose alcohol-cocaine addictions spiraled out of control. Then there was receiver Billy Parks, anti-Nixon, anti–Vietnam War zealot to a near violent degree, an idealist who once declined to play, claiming a sore knee, upset that good friend Tody Smith had been deactivated that week.

"Put Parks' brain in a hummingbird," said teammate Pat Toomay, "and it would still fly backward."

One of Landry's enduring foibles was mangling names of coaches and players, including some of his own. Mick Tinglehoff emerged as "Tinglehoffer," Dick Vermeil became "Vermillion," and Jack Scarpati was referred to as "Scarpeter." He spoke of Cowboys quarterback Gary Hogeboom as "Hogebloom."

His worst name fumbling occurred after deciding Hogeboom would replace White as the starting quarterback. In a rare instance of public fluster, Landry blurted, "I've decided to go with (Phil) Pozderac," naming an offensive tackle as his choice.

Landry maintained superb physical condition before his death from cancer in 2000 at age 75. Randy White recalled a stunning example of Landry's fitness during his rookie season.

Running up and down a small mountain became a training camp ritual at Thousand Oaks before or after practice. Players and some coaches did it to test endurance, conditioning, and because Landry wanted them to. The peak had been conquered years ago by actor John Wayne disguised as a marine. He used the site to film the flag-planting ceremony in the movie *Sands of Iwo Jima.*

White ran the mountain on a day Landry joined Randy's group. At 6'2" and about 200 well-muscled pounds, the coach looked in shape to White. But the old fellow was nearly bald and almost 50, more than twice Randy's age. Why would he embarrass himself against nimble youth?

Landry took off like a mountain goat. White took off and stalled. Landry finished before White made it halfway down. Not only that, he stood at the bottom of the mountain, barely out of breath while checking his watch to time stragglers.

"Geez," White thought to himself. "How am I going to make this team? I can't even out-run the coach."

Landry made spare use of humor, but when he did, a dry wit surfaced. At the sight of three bearded, scruffy reporters advancing for postpractice remarks he said, "Every time I see you guys coming I want to call security." Or when Tony Dorsett got bucked off a horse, Landry greeted him the next day with a reference to his childhood movie era, "Well, if it isn't Hopalong Cassidy."

Yet in '65, as Landry began his sixth season with the Cowboys, his persona remained hidden by his unflinching composure. During his remaining 23 years on the job, agonizing defeat and glorious victory slowly, but eventually, raised the curtain on the man inside.

# Getting It Half Right

For the first time in their brief existence the Cowboys proved (in 1965) that they were capable of completing a season without a losing record. Of course, they weren't mature enough to close with a winning one, either.

Only in retrospect would modest progress from a 7–7 finish assume historical significance. This would be the last year the Cowboys spent as an irrelevant title contender for the next two decades. Many links of a championship chain had been connected and 12 months later they would begin an NFL record run of 20 consecutive winning seasons.

But not yet, not before enduring an exasperating series of minipeaks and improbable deep valleys in '65. Four dizzy events were reminiscent of how one-time Philadelphia coach Joe Kuharich described the trade of two starting quarterbacks.

"It's rare, but not unusual," he said.

Things that happened to the Cowboys were both, since no other team ever repeated most of them. The list included...

- Combining with Green Bay to set an NFL record for negative passing yards in a single game that likely will never be approached, much less broken.
- Seeing Don Meredith commit virtual athletic suicide in a ghastly performance against Cleveland.
- Qualifying for their first playoff and being routed by a running back turned emergency quarterback.
- Tom Landry deciding which of three quarterbacks to stick with at midseason.

The Cowboys had assembled a nice array of defensive talent, although most remained in embryonic form. The defense sported Bob

Lilly and George Andrie in the line, Chuck Howley and Dave Edwards at linebacker, Mel Renfro and Cornell Green in the secondary.

The offense was less steady. Rookies Craig Morton and Jerry Rhome arrived to challenge Meredith, who had Bob Hayes and Frank Clarke as best-threat receivers and Don Perkins at fullback, but only Ralph Neely and Dave Manders as solid offensive line support.

At season's end the year before, after Meredith survived 58 sacks and was hit as many times or more, Landry told his quarterback he'd provide better protection in the future.

"Promise?" replied the battered passer.

Meredith often played courageously with a variety of injuries. He once threw a touchdown pass against Washington after being smoked by a blitzing linebacker. Asked if he noticed his quarterback was groggy, Landry said, "No. I'm so used to seeing him that way. I can't tell the difference anymore."

A 2–0 start quickly turned sour. Meredith hit a 37.7 percent passing slump. Landry shuttled Morton and Rhome in Game 4 only to see the defense join Meredith in a 35–24 loss to Philadelphia. Rhome started the next Sunday in Cleveland, followed by a Morton-Rhome shuttle and then Meredith to mop up another loss. The season was already on the brink when Landry named Morton to start against Green Bay.

The game was played in County Stadium during an era when the Packers split their home schedule between Milwaukee and hometown Lambeau Field. It stands as the most statistically weird result in Cowboys' history, and maybe the NFL as well. Total passing yardage for both teams: *minus 11 yards.*

Morton completed 10 of 20 passes for 61 yards and was trapped nine times for losses of 62 yards. This left him with a net of minus one passing yard. Bart Starr, an elite 10-year veteran on the eventual NFL championship team, fared even worse despite a 13–3 victory.

Starr hit only four of 19 for 42 yards, lost 52 being sacked, and wound up with a net of minus 10 passing yards. The combined negative passing

**DID YOU KNOW . . .** That Pete Gent, author of *North Dallas Forty*, caught 43 passes during the 1965 and 1966 seasons? He never felt his roster spot was secure, however, saying once, "A paranoid is a guy with all the facts."

*Defensive back Mel Renfro (No. 20), here against the Steelers in Super Bowl X, was one of many young standout players who joined the Cowboys in the mid-1960s.*

yardage for two teams remains an NFL record more than 40 years later. "I can't remember when our offense had a tougher time," Starr said.

Landry flip-flopped to start Meredith the next week. Meredith rewarded Landry's faith with a dreadful performance in a loss against lowly Pittsburgh. Landry cried in the locker room. The team sunk to a 2–5 record. Landry spoke of devoting the rest of the season to developing Morton and Rhome. With everyone prepared to bury Meredith, Landry reversed and named Meredith as his starter for the last seven games.

"I know that there are many who disagree, but I still feel firmly that my decision in 1965 to stick with Don was the most important one made in the team's history and [that it] led directly to the conference championships in 1966 and 1967," Landry said when Meredith retired after the '68 season.

Meredith made Landry look smart by leading consecutive victories prior to a visit by Eastern Conference power Cleveland. Games against the Browns and world champion Packers during the '60s were season highlights. A test against the best measured the young Cowboys' strength.

A first-time, capacity-plus crowd of about 80,000 jammed the Cotton Bowl, hopeful that the Cowboys could conquer an NFL aristocrat. And they came close twice in the fourth quarter, once as close as the Cleveland 1-yard line. Star-crossed Meredith reduced both threats to a horrendous tease.

Behind 24–17 with 10 minutes left, Dallas had a first down at the Cleveland one when Meredith made an astounding decision. He faked a handoff to Perkins and fired a bullet pass into the end zone where it was tipped and intercepted by grateful linebacker Vince Costello. Disbelief swept the stadium. So did an avalanche of boos.

A turnover gave Meredith a second chance. Redemption appeared within his grasp from the Cleveland 24 with one minute and some change left. He had time to save the game and himself. But salvation in any form lay beyond Meredith's reach. He threw another interception at the 11 to lock the score at 24–17.

Gary Cartwright of *The Dallas Morning News* immortalized Meredith with a classic lead on his game story, "Outlined against a gray November sky, the Four Horsemen rode again. You know them: Famine, Death, Famine, and Meredith."

The Cowboys rebounded with a three-game winning streak to qualify for the since-abandoned and unlamented Playoff Bowl, postseason fluff pitting conference runners-up against each other. Vince Lombardi acidly referred to the event as the Loser's Bowl, but to the young Cowboys, their first playoff of any description was a big deal.

That is, until they had to play Baltimore in Miami. With John Unitas injured and out, running-back-turned-quarterback Tom Matte led the Colts to a 35–3 rout of the humiliated Cowboys.

"It was a real team effort," Landry declared. "I'll say that."

Team effort was destined to improve dramatically. So would team play, which produced spectacular victory and agonizing defeat over the next five years. The reign of next year's champions was about to begin.

# Mister Cowboy

The Cowboys began their ascent to consistent title threat in 1966 as Bob Lilly emerged as the NFL's premier defensive tackle. Coach Tom Landry predicted that Lilly would elevate himself beyond even that lofty distinction.

Landry had already hailed Lilly as the "best tackle in the league right now." His updated praise went further.

"In a few years," he said, "Lilly will establish himself as the best defensive *lineman* in the league.

"No one in the league is quicker than Lilly. Henry Jordan [Green Bay] would be the only one you could compare with Lilly. But what you tend to forget about Lilly is that he's tremendously strong. You can overpower Jordan with a strong block, but you can't handle Lilly."

Lilly was now playing to his pedigree as the Cowboys' first draft choice (No. 1 in '61) and a two-time All–Southwest Conference defensive end at TCU, where his disruptive style earned the "Purple Cloud" nickname. He would eventually play a club record 196 consecutive games, start 194 of them, earn seven All-Pro and 11 Pro Bowl honors, and become the first Cowboy inducted into the Ring of Honor and Pro Football Hall of Fame.

More elite recognition included being named to the NFL's 75th Anniversary Team, the AFL-NFL 25th Anniversary Team, and induction into the College Football Hall of Fame. And he had to qualify despite competing against double- and triple-team blocking. Lilly was one of a kind, which was Landry's consistent point.

"A man like that comes along once in a lifetime," said Landry, who issued compliments sparingly. "He's something a little more than great. Nobody is better than Lilly."

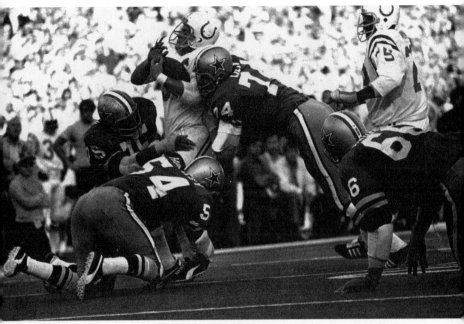

*Bob Lilly (74), here with Chuck Howley (54) and Jethro Pugh (75) tackling a Colt
running back in Super Bowl V, was the first Cowboy draft choice and the first
Cowboy inducted into the Pro Football Hall of Fame.*

Lilly was a small-town West Texan born in Throckmorton who grew
tall and trim in manhood. He stood 6'5" and weighed an almost-slim 270
pounds, but never more. Once he gained five pounds to help offset the
ever-increasing size of opposing linemen, and promptly shed them. He
said the extra weight made him feel too slow and heavy.

Lilly's strength developed early through working summers on the
family farm. Up at 5:30 AM, he drove a tractor until dark six days a
week.

"I felt guilty when I got off the tractor to get a drink of water," he
recalled. "Dad let me have Sunday off and I thought that was the greatest thing in the world. I used to haul hay and by the time I was a
freshman in high school, I could pull the motor out of a flatbed V-8."

Strength-related legends endeared Lilly to the Cowboys. As a TCU
freshman he allegedly lifted a Volkswagen—one end at a time—onto a
sidewalk. This feat contrasted sharply with Lilly's self-assessment in high
school, "I was a clumsy kid…kept falling down a lot…got my nose broken

**TOP TEN**

All-Time Cowboys Defensive Linemen

1.  Bob Lilly
2.  Randy White
3.  Harvey Martin
4.  Too Tall Jones
5.  George Andrie
6.  Jethro Pugh
7.  Jim Jeffcoat
8.  Larry Cole
9.  Charles Haley
10. Tony Tolbert

in the first practice I ever had...might have said the heck with it right there if I hadn't been afraid of everybody in school calling me a coward."

During the first two-plus seasons of Lilly's NFL career there were doubts he'd mature into more than an average defensive end. Sure, he'd made the All-Rookie Team, mainly because few options existed. Lilly floundered at end, as he had in the College All-Star camp under Coach Otto Graham. The old All-Pro quarterback described Lilly as one of his "biggest disappointments."

Lilly didn't disappoint as much as make the Cowboys ponder why he didn't play better. It finally dawned on coaches that perhaps his talent didn't suit the position. They moved Lilly to tackle early in '63, to the regret of the next generation of opposing guards, centers, and quarterbacks.

"Lilly is so quick and smart," said Bob Griese, the Miami passer, "he's almost impossible to fool. He's not enormous physically but he's strong enough so that there isn't any use arguing with him if he gets hold of your jersey. You just fall whichever way Lilly wants."

After playing his first pro game against Lilly, guard Tom Luken of Philadelphia said, "I learned more today than in nine years of high school and college football. He's everything they say he is."

And tackle was everything that matched Lilly's talent and temperament.

"I didn't have the freedom [at end that] I have at defensive tackle," he explained. "I felt more at home at tackle. There's a lot more action at that position. You don't have to hold up and wait for reverses and quarterback rolls and all that. Being head up on a man and being able to play him is my kind of football.

"I never wanted to play anywhere but on the defensive line. On the line you have the greatest challenge in the world. It's a physical battle on every play, but it's also a battle of minds and wills."

Lilly was the antithesis of the roughhouse, gap-toothed stereotype pass rusher. There was a gentle side to his nature. His hobby was photography, and he was good enough at it to stage one-man shows of his work and have others featured in a picture book collection.

Further, he played a hard and clean game with more finesse than force. Coaches wondered how much chaos Lilly would create if he lost his temper and played mad. The answer is, probably not as much, because Lilly's superb instincts would've been distracted by emotion.

Lilly could vent. Disgusted with losing Super Bowl V to Baltimore in the final seconds, 16–13, he threw his helmet 30 yards upfield. That left-handed toss epitomized the collective wounds from a fifth consecutive playoff defeat.

Nor was he always docile. He caused a training camp crisis during this period of depression. En route to the preseason base in Thousand Oaks, a frustrated Lilly landed in Los Angeles, caught a flight back to Dallas and said he was retiring. Tex Schramm rushed to Lilly's side and brought him back—the only instance in Cowboys history where management hustled to such an extreme to placate a player.

Such was the measure of respect for the franchise icon, the player who upon retirement in 1974 became Mister Cowboy. Landry had the last word on Lilly.

"There won't be another Bob Lilly in my time," he said. "You're observing a man who will become a legend."

**DID YOU KNOW . . .** That Bob Lilly never missed a game, playing in 196 consecutive games, which remains the club record?

# Green Bay Blues

With a first down at the Green Bay 2-yard line, game clock draining, a touchdown needed to force overtime, when composure meant the most, Coach Tom Landry's major ambition for his young Cowboys met its most daunting test.

"The whole idea," Landry had said, "is someday you'll grow up to a point you can beat the Packers."

In 1966 the Cowboys were still too immature to do it in the pinnacle game of their young lives—the NFL championship before a 75,504 sellout in the Cotton Bowl. Their bid to tie expired amid juvenile errors at the cusp of the Green Bay end zone.

Beginning on this New Year's date, five consecutive seasons would end with variations of the same theme. The Cowboys found inventive ways to lose playoffs—narrowly in the fading seconds, twice quickly and by huge margins, and once again via quirky failure at the 1-yard line in a Super Bowl. This became the first of that wrenching number.

The Packers were a dynasty in progress during the 1960s, three NFL titles ('61, '62, '65) already in hand and two more ('66, '67) en route. The Cowboys were seven years old, comparative infants, virtual playoff rookies, and they wanted to beat Green Bay in a meaningful game. Their clash pitted former New York Giants assistants Vince Lombardi and Landry. It also qualified the winner for the inaugural NFL-AFL playoff to settle pro football supremacy two weeks later in Los Angeles.

The Green Bay series had assumed consequence as a rite of passage for the Cowboys. Victory over the Packers would confirm them as a bona fide contender, even if it occurred during preseason. Landry often played starters into the fourth quarter to underline the value of exhibitions against Green Bay. Another capacity crowd, a 75,504 replica of the playoff audience, reflected the intensity of interest in August when Dallas beat the Packers in a no-count scrum, 21–3.

The Cowboys otherwise were 1–4 against the Packers in exhibitions and 0–3 during regular season. They were closing the gap, but had they at least drawn even?

Interest in the title game was enormous. It had been percolating in Dallas since 1960 when few knew or cared that the ragtag expansion team practiced in a dingy minor league baseball stadium. An unwelcome human presence disturbed the homesteading rodent population. To rebuke the intruders, during overnight hours rats gnawed holes in the players' equipment.

That same founding year the Cowboys flew home from New York in a state of jubilation. They had tied the Giants, 31–31, and reveled in their first and only nondefeat of a season destined to end 0–11–1.

Two fans, double the number that normally greeted the team at Love Field, met their charter plane. The pair waved a sign that said: "Well Done, Cowboys."

## TRIVIA

**Who was the first Cowboy to score eight touchdowns both rushing and receiving?**

*Answers to the trivia questions are on pages 163–164.*

"Well, we're making progress," said Landry, noting an incremental increase in customer attention.

The '66 Cowboys made the same return flight from Yankee Stadium in an equally blissful state. They'd beaten the Giants again, 17–7. But now they were returning to Dallas as first-time champions of the Eastern Conference with a 10–3–1 record. For kicker Danny Villanueva, veteran of losing teams in Los Angeles and Dallas, it was a moment to savor.

"Seven years, seven years on the bottom," Villanueva kept repeating to seat mate Jerry Rhome. "Seven years of being a loser, and now look where we are."

Rhome glanced out the window.

"About over Memphis," he reckoned.

Owner Clint Murchison Jr. announced over the intercom he would host a party for players at an upscale club in North Park, the newest and largest shopping center in Dallas developed by Ray Nasher. Murchison added one requirement to his invitation, "Have fun and stay as long as

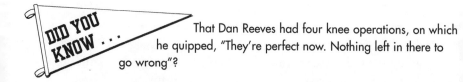

you like. All I ask is that everyone clear out before 9:00 in the morning. That's when the Christmas shoppers show up."

Moments later, as the plane glided toward landing, Murchison spoke again over the intercom. "Welcome to Dallas, former home of the Kansas City Chiefs," he jabbed.

The thunderous welcoming crowd numbered an estimated 10,000, while thousands more futilely circled Love Field searching for a parking space. Players walked a gauntlet of whistling, cheering fans. This indeed was progress.

The game exceeded its hype as a match between established royalty and challenger to the throne. *Chicago Tribune* sports editor George Strickler, who'd seen them all, described what transpired as "the most dramatic championship game in history." Much of Strickler's opinion evolved from the Cowboys' refusal to fold under an immediate barrage by the Packers.

Quarterback Don Meredith, who sang in the huddle to relieve tension ("I been down so long it looks up to me"), rallied from an early 14–0 hole. The deficit occurred so early—opening touchdown drive by Green Bay, touchdown runback of the subsequently fumbled kickoff— that Meredith's offense hadn't run a play with the game less than four minutes old.

Dallas tied at 14–14, fell behind 21–14, inched to within 21–17 at halftime, got close again at 21–20, saw Green Bay stretch its lead to 34–20, trimmed that to 34–27, and with 1:52 left had that first down at the Packers' 2-yard line. Those 72 inches might as well have been 72 miles. Catastrophe wore many faces. The goal line series failed.

Dan Reeves gained one yard on a first down plunge. On the second down, tackle Jim Boeke jumped the snap count, and a sideline camera caught Landry whipping his head around with a grimace. Now it was second from the 6-yard line. Meredith threw a swing pass to Reeves that looked good for a touchdown with a lead blocker, and Reeves matched against one Green Bay defender.

But Reeves dropped the ball because his vision was blurred. His left eyeball had been scraped on the earlier carry, a handicap he didn't mention to Meredith. Now it was third down, and Meredith passed to tight end Pettis Norman standing in the end zone. But his pass was low. Norman retreated to the 2-yard line to catch it and was touched down there.

"I didn't have faith in my call," Meredith admitted later. "If there's one slogan Landry pounded into us, it's 'Never give the defense more credit than it deserves.' The play is designed on the premise that the linebacker on that side [Dave Robinson] will not cover Pettis. I guess I couldn't really believe it.

"So I hesitated when I threw the ball, looking for Robinson. That's why it was low. If I'd thrown it chest high, Pettis could've waltzed in for a touchdown."

Now it was fourth down and no one noticed Bob Hayes on the field. Frank Clarke, a superior blocker, routinely replaced Hayes on possessions

*Mel Renfro defends Jim Taylor in the Cowboys 34–27 loss to the Packers in the 1966 NFL championship game, actually played in January of 1967.*

inside the 10-yard line, but unaccountably still stood on the sideline. When Meredith rolled right, Robinson shot past the stationary Hayes and forced Meredith to wing a lob-and-hope pass into the end zone. Safety Tom Brown of the Packers intercepted to claim the final Cowboys error.

"It was my mistake for not noticing Hayes and sending him off," said Meredith. "It was Hayes' mistake for not getting out of there on his own. It was Tom's mistake for not sending Clarke in for him."

Irony oozed from the 34–27 loss after the AFL qualified Kansas City as its rep in the World Championship Game. Had the Cowboys advanced they would have played their former intercity Dallas rival. As matters turned, the Packers beat the Chiefs handily (35–10) and Lombardi said afterward that the Cowboys were a better team than Kansas City.

Lombardi's praise was genuine. However, it bore no future currency. Unspoken by Lombardi was the ongoing fact that the Cowboys weren't better than his Packers. The gap between them would be exposed soon enough on an ice floe in Green Bay.

# The Ice Bowl

(*"A cold air mass moving down from Canada will bring with it more fresh cold air."* Forecast for Dec. 31, 1967, from the National Weather Service in Green Bay.)

The Cowboys awoke on the morning of the NFL championship game against Green Bay in an Appleton motel, 35 miles from Lambeau Field. Overnight it appeared to have drifted to the Arctic Circle.

Or so it sounded when the wake-up call operator delivered the time and temperature in a chirpy voice.

"The lady said, 'Good morning, it's 7:00 and the temperature is 14 degrees,'" George Andrie recalled. "Then she paused for effect and said...'below zero.'"

Andrie felt this chilly news was fodder to prank roommate Bob Lilly.

"I hollered at Lilly and said, 'Hey, Bob, watch this.' I took a glass of water and tossed it against the inside of the window. The water turned to ice, froze solid, before it could drip down to the windowsill."

Lee Roy Jordan received the same wake-up call. Jordan wasn't sure he'd heard the message correctly.

"Then the phone rang again and it was one of our players, and he said, 'Did you hear what the damn temperature is?' All I could do was go to the window and look outside. I just stared. I wanted to see what [14] below looked like," Jordan said.

"The motel where we stayed was sort of horseshoe shaped. From my angle I could see most of the other rooms in the place. In almost every window I could see someone like me—a Dallas football player staring outside, wondering what it would feel like when we finally went out there."

It would feel different from 24 hours earlier when the Cowboys limbered up at Lambeau Field. They pranced on Saturday under relatively balmy conditions—18 degrees above zero, no wind, firm enough footing and light fog.

Steam rose from beneath the turf where Coach Vince Lombardi spent $80,000 installing a heating grid to prevent the surface from freezing. The warm vapor was reminiscent of an eerie scene from *The Hound of the Baskervilles* with Sherlock Holmes and Dr. Watson tramping through the moors. Yet the Cowboys were pleased with the track.

"If we have another day like this it will be ideal," said Chuck Howley, an oblique reference to the Cowboys' superior speed that the onrushing Arctic blast negated.

Instead they got a day like no other. The temperature inched to minus 13 degrees by noon, still the coldest December 31 in Green Bay history. Fierce north gusts sent the wind chill factor plummeting into numbing minus 30s. Until then, the coldest NFL championship game occurred in 1945 when hometown Cleveland beat Washington, 15–14, in five degree (above) temperature.

Lambeau Field sold out anyway. A crowd of 50,861 gathered, most outfitted for a polar expedition, others wrapped in sleeping bags, many fortified for warmth with flasks containing high-octane spirits. Each breath from the stands sent a plume of steam into the air.

Of course, there is always an exception.

"One person I'll never forget, a young woman, came to the game wearing high heels, a short cocktail dress and a lightweight jacket. Even before the game this woman turned purple," said a Green Bay fan. "I'm sure that she was from Dallas."

The brutal elements treated others worse. Four fans suffered heart attacks at the stadium. Fourteen made it on their own to hospitals for treatment of exposure. In the TV booth whiskey-laced coffee froze before the kickoff. Frank Gifford opened his commentary by saying, "I just took a bite of coffee."

## TRIVIA

Who said, when reminded that his first NFL start would be against L.A Rams' star defensive end Deacon Jones, famous for being agile, mobile, and hostile: "Well, so am I"?

*Answers to the trivia questions are on pages 163–164.*

## All-Time Cowboys Linebackers

1. Chuck Howley
2. Lee Roy Jordan
3. Bob Breunig
4. Eugene Lockhart
5. Dave Edwards
6. Ken Norton
7. D. D. Lewis
8. Randall Godfrey
9. Dexter Coakley
10. Jerry Tubbs

Nor did the band play, for fear lips would stick to metal on frozen instruments. Officials used verbal commands instead of whistles for the same reason. With the game only minutes old, Jordan noticed another surreal scene on the Cowboys' sideline.

"Tom had icicles an inch and a half long sticking down from either nostril," Lee Roy said. "He looked a little...weird."

The game looked equally weird. Players took mincing steps in search of traction. Both teams averaged less than three yards rushing per carry. Passing was like throwing a frozen pumpkin. Every punt sounded like a rifle shot. Lombardi's heating grid became a glorious casualty, as Walt Garrison noted in describing the texture of Lambeau Field, "Like walking on asphalt. Harder than Chinese arithmetic."

Early action appeared borrowed from the previous NFL title match when Green Bay duplicated a 14–0 lead on touchdown passes from Bart Starr to Boyd Dowler. The Cowboys rallied, thanks to a decision by defensive coordinator Ernie Stautner, who refused to allow his linemen to wear gloves. Gloves might impair your grip with a chance to recover a fumble, he advised them.

True to Stautner's advice, Andrie ran seven yards to score with a Starr bobble created by a hit from Willie Townes. A Danny Villanueva field goal made it 14–10 at the half, and Dan Reeves threw a 50-yard half-back pass to Lance Rentzel as the fourth opened. Dallas still led 17–14 with 4:50 left and Green Bay backed to its 32-yard line.

*The Packers' Bart Starr scores the winning touchdown in the Ice Bowl, perhaps pro football's most famous game.*

The players by now were beyond numbed. Jethro Pugh began to hallucinate, recalling how his mother fussed at her children when they went outside and got their feet wet.

"I swear," said Pugh, "I heard her say, 'Jethro, what are you doing out in that weather, you fool?'"

The outcome eventually hung on one play: Green Bay at the Dallas 1-yard line with no time outs and 0:16 on the clock. The Packers faced third down. An incomplete pass would leave time enough to attempt a tying field goal. A failed running play would likely consume the final seconds with the Cowboys dawdling to get up or line up before game's end.

"I thought Starr might roll out and throw or run, depending on what he saw," Landry said.

Starr did neither. He and Lombardi conferred on the sideline and opted to win or lose on a quarterback sneak. They won, 21–17, with a gamble that was considered brilliant because it worked. Starr fell into the end zone behind blocks on Pugh by Jerry Kramer and Ken Bowman with 0:13 remaining.

Someone asked Ralph Neely if he'd seen Lombardi after the game, and how he looked because the temperature had dipped to 20 degrees below zero and the wind chill to minus 41 degrees.

"He had a smile on his face," Neely replied. "Whether or not it was frozen, I can't say."

Owner Clint Murchison Jr., normally the source of a wry quote, had no pun to fit his mood. "The day wasn't too cold if you won," he said.

The decision behind Starr's sneak left some Cowboys coaches incredulous. They considered the sneak tactically unsound. Jerry Tubbs was aghast when reminded the Packers did it without benefit of a timeout.

"A quarterback sneak, how the hell can they go for a lousy quarterback sneak?" added Stautner.

"It was a dumb call. But now it's a great play," said Landry in a rare critique of an opponent.

Andrie subscribed to a mock conspiracy theory to account for the ice rink surface. "That...Lombardi...he turned off his machine," he alleged.

Landry found the proper words to describe his anguished post–Ice Bowl team. It had played gallantly and honorably under miserable conditions but again, not quite good enough.

"You can tell the real Cowboys," Landry later informed a banquet audience in San Antonio. "They're the ones with the frozen fingers and broken hearts."

# Next Year's Champions

In his book, *Dallas Cowboys: Pro or Con,* columnist Sam Blair found a scene that described the image that would attach to Coach Tom Landry's team for the next three seasons. He found it in a cartoon by Charles Schulz, creator of the comic strip *Peanuts.*

Tacked to a bulletin board near the assistant coaches' desk was a sketch of Linus, elbows on the table, chin in hand, gazing at the world with this lament, "There's no heavier burden than a great potential."

Darrell Royal, who coached three national championships at the University of Texas, had an original spin on the same thought.

"Potential means you ain't done it yet," Royal said.

The Cowboys hadn't done it against Green Bay in 1966 and '67 title games. Nor would they do it in 1968, '69, or '70 playoffs up to and including Super Bowl V. Five consecutive postseason defeats earned them the mocking brand of Next Year's Champions.

"The Dallas Cowboys are terrific in summer stock and tryouts in Bridgeport but despite their glitter and promise they can't cut it on Broadway," agreed New York pundit Larry Merchant.

Frustration peaked in part because the Cowboys were ahead of the curve in finding talent in obscure sites, but behind annually on playoff scoreboards. Small black colleges received special emphasis. Scouts found players like Jethro Pugh (Elizabeth City State) and Pettis Norman (Johnson C. Smith) in North Carolina, Rayfield Wright (Fort Valley State) in Georgia, and Herb Scott (Virginia Union).

The Cowboys even spent $20,000 on a Kicking Karavan, a six-week, 10,000-mile odyssey through 28 cities. Former NFL kicker Ben Agajanian was among the judges; his claim to fame was that a long pro career hadn't been impeded by his loss of the toes on his right foot in an accident. This accounted for Agajanian wearing a smaller shoe on his kicking foot.

Open to all comers, the Kicking Karavan drew a wild assortment of wannabe prospects. One was a bus driver. He left his passengers parked, missed one kick with a change purse rattling around his waist, returned to the bus, and drove away.

The wife of another wayward kicker complained, "He's been making me hold the ball, and all my fingernails are gone." The worst volunteer made eight attempts—hitting the ball three times with his knee and five times with his shin.

One of the failures noticed Agajanian's footwear and said, "I guess I need one of those short shoes like you got. Where do you get them?"

"First," Agajanian replied, "you take your toes off."

Nothing significant evolved from the Kicking Karavan. Neither did the '68 season produce the anticipated result, despite a best-ever 12–2 record and Meredith at his career peak. At least he was, until playoffs began in Cleveland against a team the Cowboys had beaten four consecutive times and 12 months earlier by a 52–14 post-season margin. Meredith threw three interceptions, made only 43 yards passing, and gave way to Morton in the second half. The underdog Browns romped, 31–20, consigning Dallas to the ignominy of another Playoff Bowl.

"This is my most disappointing day, because we never had a club that could go all the way before," said Landry.

"A whole year shot in two and one-half hours," groaned Schramm, who tearfully embraced Meredith on the sideline at game's end. Neither knew they were hugging each other good-bye. Meredith would retire in the coming months at age 31, in effect accepting a conclusion he spoke about years earlier.

"Sometimes," he'd said, "when I'm lying on the ground at Yankee Stadium or someplace and some guy like Sam Huff is pounding my poor, thin body, I tell myself, 'Dandy, why did you ever take up this career? Why

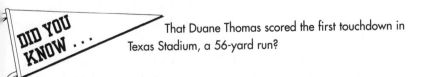

DID YOU KNOW . . . That Duane Thomas scored the first touchdown in Texas Stadium, a 56-yard run?

# TRIVIA

**What was Craig Morton's real first name?**

*Answers to the trivia questions are on pages 163–164.*

don't you get a decent job? You're too nice a person for this to be happening to. Why don't you go back to East Texas where you belong? Let the other fellows play football. You don't need it.'"

Tough fullback Don Perkins preceded Meredith in retirement; he, too, at 31. Hence the '69 season opened with a different offensive look, especially with the arrival of NFL Rookie-of-the-Year-to-be Calvin Hill, a stunning No. 1 draft choice for a divinity student from Yale.

However, the final results were nearly identical. The Morton-led Cowboys finished 11–2–1 and lost to Cleveland again in a first-round playoff, 38–14. The only difference this time was that they lost at home, Mike Clark whiffed an onside kickoff attempt, and all were booed vigorously by halftime. Ahead lay further humiliation, a 31–0 loss to Los Angeles in the Playoff Bowl, or as Lee Roy Jordan called it, "The Toilet Bowl."

Ralph Neely expressed the level of frustration. It was well nigh off the chart. "Any time you lose four years in a row, it has to have an adverse effect. I think you've got to come back and fight it, because you're a professional. But you begin a soul searching," he admitted.

"If you keep getting disappointments, you start wondering, *Is it really worth it?* You think, *Well, maybe I'll do something else.* About the time you start thinking that, you think, *Well, I'm damn sure not a quitter.* So, you hang in there."

The Cowboys fought back in '70, a season as strange as it was enchanting. Most of the struggle was uphill from 5–4 after their *Monday Night Football* debut against St. Louis in the Cotton Bowl. With Meredith an embarrassed witness in the television booth, the Cowboys were blanked during the regular season for the first time in franchise history, 38–0.

Late in the rout the former quarterback heard the crowd offer familiar chants with a reverse twist. Instead of the "We Want Morton!" chorus he endured for years, Dandy listened to boo-birds yell, "We Want Meredith!" To which he replied, "No way are you getting me down there."

An enigmatic rookie then sparked a revival that coincided with a St. Louis collapse. Tailback Duane Thomas, a Who's He? No. 1 draft choice in place of an injured Hill, and a suddenly suffocating defense lifted Dallas to a first place 10–4 finish. The Cowboys won their last five regular season games, allowing only 15 points in the last four, then won playoffs by scores of 5–0 and 17–10 to qualify for Super Bowl V against Baltimore.

The fatal flaw was lack of a passing threat. In fairness to Morton, he played on with a damaged right shoulder that required postseason surgery. Medics transplanted a tendon from his foot to stabilize the injury, sparking a lame joke that when Morton caught athlete's foot, he scratched his shoulder. No one laughed when his overthrow led to Baltimore's winning points in Super Bowl V.

Thomas had followed Hill as NFL Rookie of the Year and charmed the Super Bowl media in Miami with mystical viewpoints on any and all subjects. About how he felt playing in the ultimate game, "If it was the ultimate game," said Duane, "they wouldn't be playing it next year."

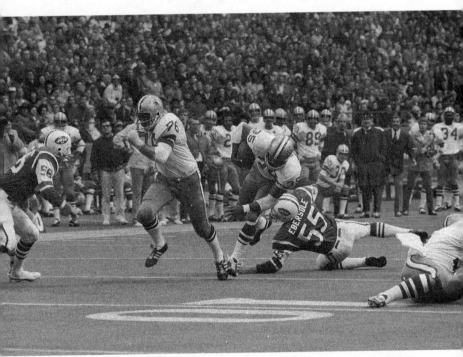

*Calvin Hill, here in action against the Jets in 1969, added punch to a struggling Cowboys offense in the late 1960s. He became the Cowboys first 1,000-yard rusher.*

Or what he was thinking when found sitting on the beach, hands wrapped around knees, peering intently out to sea, "New Zealand."

Why New Zealand?

"It sounds like a nice place to retire."

Everything went haywire in Super Bowl V. A combined 11 turnovers—six interceptions and five fumbles—got the event nicknamed "The Blooper Bowl." The Colts scored on a tipped pass covering 75 yards. Cowboy linebacker Chuck Howley became the only member of the losing team named MVP.

Still, the Cowboys were ahead 13–6 and in lock-away shape when Thomas fumbled at the Colts' 1-yard line. Center Dave Manders recovered, but officials mistakenly gave possession to Baltimore. The outcome climaxed when Morton's too-high pass skipped off Dan Reeves' hands into an interception at the Dallas 28. A 32-yard field goal by Jim O'Brien with five seconds left the Cowboys with a crushing 16–13 defeat.

Jim Murray, celebrated columnist of the *Los Angeles Times,* wrote a eulogy to the team that had been spooked in five consecutive playoffs.

"This team doesn't need a coach," went Murray's column. "It needs a witch."

## TRIVIA

**Who said, "Someone once asked my wife who played center for the Dallas Cowboys. She came and asked me"?**

*Answers to the trivia questions are on pages 163–164.*

# Captain America

En route to *Monday Night Football* fame with nasally impaired Howard Cosell, freshly retired Don Meredith had returned to training camp when he saw the Cowboys' future at quarterback. He didn't have to look far to find Craig Morton.

But Meredith's eyes were fixed on someone else. In a confidential aside he warned Morton of a threatening shadow. Meredith sensed the starting job Morton inherited from him in 1969 was already under siege.

"I tried to make it a joke," Meredith recalled. "But I said, 'Craig, I'm glad it's you instead of me against this guy because anyone who takes a vacation and comes to two-a-days has got to be a little weird. He's gonna get your job.'"

Meredith was right about the scrambling, 27-year-old rookie with a wife, three children, and the only crew cut in camp.

Roger Staubach did get Morton's job, and it took him less than three seasons. The Cowboys got the quarterback who helped them become champions, and that didn't take long, either.

Staubach had been a training camp curiosity since he twice spent his military leave from the navy to practice with the Cowboys in California. As the NFL's oldest rookie and in theory four years behind Morton in development, his task appeared the equivalent of creating a pro career in the space of a two-minute drill.

Interest in Staubach had bubbled since 1964 when the Cowboys drafted him on the 10th round as a future choice, a practice the NFL later abandoned. Bob Hayes (7th) and Jerry Rhome (13th) also were taken that year as juniors in college. Both would join the team the next season. Staubach by contrast faced four years of active duty as a navy officer.

**DID YOU KNOW ...** That Roger Staubach attended New Mexico Military Institute before he entered the Naval Academy?

Staubach wasn't entirely football-free during his military service. He kept his arm in semishape throwing footballs the Cowboys mailed to him on demand. He even played one season for a navy base team, which a bewildered Tom Landry heard about during a stressful pre-game hour.

Morton was hurt for the regular season opener against St. Louis. Staubach's starting debut as a middle-aged rookie occurred in his first NFL game. On the night before the Cotton Bowl kickoff, Staubach tried to cheer a worried Landry by reminding the coach that he wasn't totally inexperienced.

"Coach, do you realize that a year ago today I was the starting quarterback for the Pensacola Naval Air Station Goshawks? We were playing Middle Tennessee State. And here I am," he trilled, "ready to start against the Cardinals tomorrow."

Landry blinked, sighed, and walked away without a word.

With Landry calling plays, the Cowboys won (24–3) as Staubach threw a 75-yard touchdown pass to Lance Rentzel and scored on a 3-yard run. Morton returned thereafter as the starter, but the duel for number one supremacy had begun. It climaxed during a midseason crisis in '71.

The Cowboys stood 4–3, a team riddled by self-doubt and badly in need of a leader. Two previous seasons with Morton had ended in a first-round playoff flop and a last-second loss in Super Bowl V. Landry then waffled between Morton and Staubach in '71, starting one and then the other, once resorting to a QB shuttle on alternate plays.

Landry settled on Staubach and Staubach justified Landry's decision. He led the '71 Cowboys to 10 consecutive victories that included Super Bowl VI. Comebacks became his specialty. He brought the Cowboys from behind to win 23 games in the fourth quarter, 14 of them in the final two minutes or in overtime. His list of improbable rallies was topped by the most famous play in franchise history—the 50-yard Hail Mary touchdown pass to Drew Pearson to beat Minnesota in the last minute of a 1975 playoff, 17–14.

"The one thing that will always stand out in my mind about Roger is that he never knew when it was over," said tight end Billy Joe DuPree. "At the end of the game, even if we're down by 20 points, he'll be standing there by himself trying to figure out a way we can win it."

Winning further defined Staubach. He won regular season games at a remarkable .746 (85–29) clip and was never shut out. His 11–6 playoff record included victories in Super Bowls VI and XII. He even lost in thrilling fashion when bowing to Pittsburgh, 21–17 and 35–31, in Super Bowls.

"When you talk about great quarterbacks Roger has to stand alongside Otto Graham and Johnny Unitas, all the ones I can recall," said Landry from a perspective of 40 years as an NFL player and coach. "Mainly because he was such a consistent performer and one of the great two-minute performers like Bobby Layne in his prime. I don't know of any quarterback I played against or watched that I'd rather have than Roger."

Staubach's impeccable lifestyle helped confirm the Cowboys as "America's Team," a label originated by NFL Films. The flattering term made Staubach

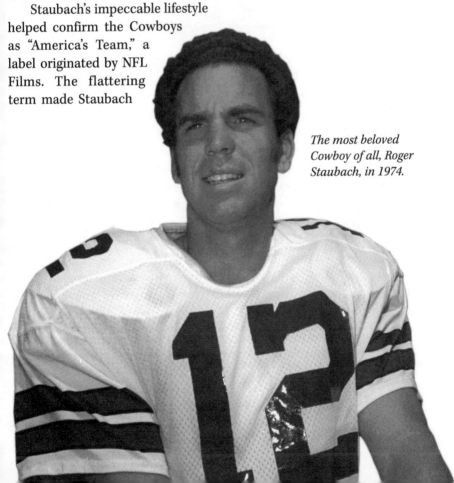

*The most beloved Cowboy of all, Roger Staubach, in 1974.*

**By the NUMBERS**

**2**—Final season national ranking of 1963 Naval Academy, quarterbacked by Staubach

**4**—Times Roger Staubach led NFL in passing yardage

**6**—Times Roger Staubach was elected to Pro Bowl

**20**—Career touchdowns scored running by Roger Staubach

**83.4**—Roger Staubach's career passing rating, the best up until that time

**153**—Career touchdown passes thrown by Roger Staubach

**1,685**—Career completions by Roger Staubach

**1985**—Year Roger Staubach was inducted into the Pro Football Hall of Fame

**2,264**—Roger Staubach's career rushing yardage

**22,700**—Roger Staubach's career passing yardage

cringe, but teammate Cliff Harris thought it fit him in a personal sense.

"The Cowboys have been conceived as America's Team," Harris said. "They were the clean-cut team. It's because of Roger. They developed *his* image because that's what he was—Captain America."

Others had a teasing take on Staubach's pristine image.

"He can play until he's 40 because he doesn't know what a hangover is," said Sonny Jurgensen, former high-living quarterback for the Washington Redskins.

Meredith elaborated on the same theme, "We're going to have to do something about this guy. He's going to ruin the image of an NFL quarterback if he doesn't start smoking, drinking, cussing, or something."

"Staubach's idea of breaking training is putting whipped cream on his pie," a local writer added.

Staubach had a lively sense of humor and was nervy enough to direct it at Landry. Once during timeout of a home game, he went to the sideline to meet Landry and get the next play. He waited and waited and...

Landry stood silent, his gaze fixed toward the hole in the roof of Texas Stadium. Staubach interrupted Landry's reverie to tease, "I always wondered where you got some of those plays."

Nor was president/general manager Tex Schramm immune from Staubach's most famous stunt, a dramatic scramble that occurred 200 feet above ground without a net. It happened one afternoon when

Staubach tired of waiting for an audience with Schramm, busy on a conference call.

Schramm's 11th story office was floor to ceiling glass on two sides with a grand view to the north and east. As Tex talked on, Staubach found a door leading outside and sidestepped along a two-foot wide ledge until he stood behind Schramm on the opposite side of the north wall glass.

When Schramm swiveled his chair in that direction, he went rigid at the sight of Staubach, legs a straddle, arms waving, a trick-or-treat grin on his face, hair blowing in the wind, and nothing behind him but air and empty space. "I gotta go," Schramm stammered into the phone. "You may not believe this but my quarterback is standing outside my office on an 11th-story ledge!"

Staubach also could poke fun at himself. Few noticed that the little finger of his passing hand was badly disfigured. It angled down and away, bent awkwardly by multiple dislocations, and bulged with calcium deposits. Someone asked why he didn't have the finger repaired.

"Oh, I don't want to do that," he protested. "It gets me in handicapped parking."

When Staubach retired after the '79 season as the NFL's No. 1 ranked all-time passer, he'd swept the board with personal honors. He won the Heisman Trophy and Maxwell Award in college, plus the Bert Bell Award in the NFL. All

## TRIVIA

**Who caught the last pass of Roger Staubach's career?**

*Answers to the trivia questions are on pages 163–164.*

are symbolic of player of the year status. He was named Most Valuable Player in Super Bowl VI, made the All–National Conference team four times, and earned six trips to the Pro Bowl.

More recognition came later. Staubach was inducted into the Ring of Honor (1983) and the Pro Football Hall of Fame (1985). Bob Ryan, editor and chief of NFL Films, supplied a fitting athletic eulogy at the conclusion of a career-highlight film of Staubach, the first that NFL Films compiled on an individual player.

"For everyone touched by Roger Staubach," went Ryan's narration, "say a fond farewell. For you and the game of football will be diminished by his absence."

# Super Bowl VI

The Cowboys won Super Bowl VI by beating Miami, the least threatening of opponents during the 1971 season, and not because the Dolphins were easy 24–3 victims. This was a year where turmoil from within became the most formidable challenger.

The road to the pinnacle game in New Orleans was littered with the distracting refuse of one player's rebellion, freak injury, indecisive coaching, and a hangover reputation for inability to win the big one. What should have been a joyous romp to the NFL pinnacle turned into a forced march with jaws clenched. The Cowboys were relieved, more than ecstatic, to win Super Bowl VI.

Unrest surfaced early and lasted. In fact, one angry issue lingered until the next summer before it was settled.

The season did include a gaudy event that preceded Super Bowl triumph. The Clint Murchison–inspired Texas Stadium was christened on October 24 with a 44–21 victory over New England. Murchison's guests included former president Lyndon B. Johnson and former first ladies Lady Bird Johnson and Mamie Eisenhower. The sellout crowd included 65,705 people.

Texas Stadium's interior was ringed by 150 luxury suites with 16 x 16 foot dimensions selling for a then-astronomical $50,000. Yet that price would in time prove a bargain. At least one midfield suite later sold for as much as $1 million. Texas Stadium's unique hole-in-the-roof design caused as much commentary, some of it in joking terms.

It's a half-Astrodome, went one description. Another saw the architecture influenced by heavenly edict. The hole in the roof allowed God to watch his team play.

Meantime, back on Earth in suburban Irving, mere mortals cheered as halfback Duane Thomas scored the first touchdown in the new playpen on a 56-yard ramble. Thomas by then was the center of a silent storm. The NFC's rookie of the year in '70 wasn't speaking, and that included refusal to answer roll call.

# TRIVIA

**What did Don Meredith say about Cowboys running back Walt Garrison during a broadcast of *Monday Night Football*?**

*Answers to the trivia questions are on pages 163–164.*

He had become mute, a resident sphinx, resentment stemming from his inability to restructure his contract. Or so it was believed. When Thomas tried to explain his complaint during a preseason rant he rambled to no effect.

However, remarks directed at Tom Landry, Tex Schramm, and Gil Brandt needed no translation. During a press conference in Dallas while the team huddled in training camp, Thomas called Landry, "a plastic man...no man at all," Schramm, "sick, demented, and dishonest," and Brandt, "a liar."

"Not bad," Schramm responded, "he got two out of three."

Thomas was an asset/problem for Landry, who bent his once inflexible rules to accommodate the moody runner. Thomas ignored dress codes for road games, skipped workouts or declined to join them in progress, snubbed teammates and coaches, and Landry tolerated the misbehavior. Players griped about a double standard, which Landry denied until the season ended when he announced henceforth there would be no more double standards.

Yet Thomas was a brilliant runner, always prepared, and never gave less than maximum effort on the field. Plus in the privacy of Landry's mind, Thomas was the threat that gave the Cowboys all-the-way potential. Therein lay the dilemma on how to handle him.

"Duane has become for the Cowboys what Russia was to Churchill: the proverbial enigma wrapped in a riddle, doused with Tabasco sauce, and stuffed in a cheese enchilada," teammate Pat Toomay analyzed.

Landry had another problem that complicated the offense and annoyed the team. He opened the season by anointing Craig Morton and Roger Staubach co-quarterbacks. One or the other started on alternate weeks. The nadir of their stalemate occurred when they shuttled on

# TRIVIA

**Who holds the Cowboys record for most appearances in playoff games?**

*Answers to the trivia questions are on pages 163–164.*

alternate plays, lost in Chicago, and the record fell to 4–3. Landry caught heat for waffling. The most stinging rebuff originated from his former quarterback.

"Landry's responsibility as head coach is to pick a quarterback," said Don Meredith from his seat in the announcing booth. "Now, after all this time, he still does not have any idea who is best. Then get another coach."

Players also were frazzled by lack of definition at such a sensitive position. "It would help to have one quarterback," said offensive tackle Ralph Neely. "Either damn one. At this point, I don't care."

When Neely broke his leg in a motorbike accident, Landry knew it would help if he had a healthy replacement. He didn't. All the reserves ailed. So Landry coaxed Tony Liscio, retired former tackle living in Dallas, into uniform. Liscio agreed and played splendidly, beginning with three games within a 12-day span over Thanksgiving.

"If anyone wants to see me," said Liscio after his first start, "I'll be in the whirlpool."

Landry finally capitulated on the quarterback issue and chose Staubach, less experienced but far more mobile than Morton. The wisdom of that choice was demonstrated three weeks later when Staubach scored on a 29-yard scramble to help beat Washington 13–0. Further evidence arrived via a 10-game winning streak through Super Bowl VI.

The game was less compelling than the prelude and postscript.

Thomas was still not speaking, which led to a weird scene on media day devoted to interviewing players. Thomas took a seat on a set of bleachers, surrounded by reporters. After a few minutes of questions that begat no answer, most writers drifted away.

All rushed back when they saw Thomas whisper to a lone hanger-on. This could be a stop-press bulletin! What did he say? The reporter had written Duane's remark. Consulting his notebook before a hushed audience, he said the actual words from Thomas were, "What time is it?"

There was enough time for past and present occupants of the White House to make pre-kickoff headlines. President Richard Nixon, a winter resident of Key Biscayne, called Don Shula with a tactical tip in case it might not have occurred to the Miami coach.

"Now the Cowboys are a good team," said Nixon, "but I still think you can hit [Paul] Warfield on that down-and-in pattern against them. You know the one."

Days later, Tom Landry received a telegram from former president and Texas native Lyndon Johnson. It read, "Tom, my prayers and my presence will be with you in New Orleans, although I have no plans to send in any plays."

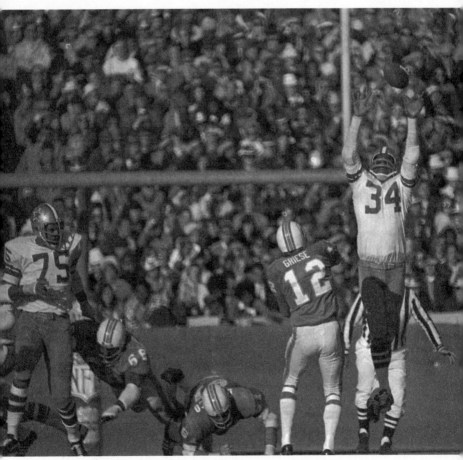

*Cowboy Cornell Green knocks down a Bob Griese pass in the Cowboys 24–3 win over Miami in Super Bowl VI, the Cowboys first NFL championship.*

Grimly determined and composed, the Cowboys made a competitive mockery of Super Bowl VI. They rushed for a record 252 yards, Staubach won the MVP award, and instead of flinging his helmet in disgust as he had 12 months earlier in Super Bowl V, Bob Lilly lit a foot-long cigar. Lilly, aided by Larry Cole, supplied one of the defensive highlights by circling a retreating Bob Griese until trapping him for a monstrous 29-yard loss.

"It was like cutting horses at a rodeo," said Cole.

"My biggest disappointment was that we never challenged," said Shula. "They completely dominated. They had the ball more than 40 minutes and we had it less than 20."

Nixon called Landry in the locker room to congratulate him and the team. "It was a bad connection but he said the offensive line did a great job," Landry replayed.

Did he say anything about the down-and-in to Warfield (4-for-39 yards receiving)?

"No," Landry said with a small smile. "When your down-and-ins aren't working, you don't mention them."

The final bizarre scene involved Thomas, thrust before rattled CBS-TV postgame announcer Tom Brookshier. "Are you fast?" Brookshier stammered. "Evidently," replied Thomas, who had former Cleveland great Jim Brown in company as an advisor. "Your weight fluctuates," observed Brookshier to no apparent purpose. "I weigh what I need to," said Thomas (an equally fascinating answer).

In this, the last game Thomas played for the Cowboys, he rushed for 95 yards on 19 carries. He rebelled again during the '72 training camp. His last act of defiance was refusing to leave his dorm room. He wound up traded to San Diego, then to Washington, where he scored a touchdown against the Cowboys in '74, and soon drifted from the NFL scene.

Those events would play out in the future. The Cowboys meantime basked in the present, no longer Next Year's Champions.

# Texas (as in Schramm)

Texas Ernest Schramm Jr. was convinced that there was nothing he couldn't do better than the knuckleheads in charge of television, sports departments, baseball, government, other NFL teams in general, and the NFL commissioner's office in particular.

Those who knew him thought he might be right.

Schramm was rarely satisfied with the status quo unless it was the flavor of J&B Scotch whiskey, for which he held an approving taste. Tex was forever thinking about how to do everything bigger, better, and with unique flair. And how to do it first-class so that when his days were done, history would record he left a mark of lasting brilliance.

Such was his announced mission when the Cowboys joined the NFL in 1960. Schramm rejected the ordinary as unacceptable. The ultimate fear of his restless mind was to be irrelevant, another face in the faceless multitude. He left modest ambition to the modest.

"I don't hide the fact that I'm history-conscious," he said. "I want the organization to be remembered in such a way that everyone who was part of it—the players, coaches, and people working in the front office—will look back and know they were part of something special, something great."

Schramm himself was someone special—opinionated, irascible, hot-tempered, stubborn, innovative but also generous, likeable, loyal, and one of the towering figures of his NFL era.

And on January 16, 1972, he *felt* extra special. His beloved Cowboys won Super Bowl VI, a thorough 24–3 romp over Miami in New Orleans. The expansion team that wore diapers 12 years ago had matured into a manly world champion. Schramm was convinced that the future promised many more Lombardi Trophies.

# TRIVIA

In which baseball park did the Cowboys conduct practices in 1960?

*Answers to the trivia questions are on pages 163–164.*

"This is just the beginning," boasted the president/general manager. "We have a young team. I can see the Cowboys becoming a dynasty...we have many championships in front of us."

Schramm's prediction turned out half right. Instead of Super Bowls in multiples, the Cowboys won one more and lost two by a total of eight points during the '70s. His status as a Mount Rushmore figure in the NFL was already assured, and confirmed in 1991 when he became the only nonplayer-coach-owner-commissioner inducted into the Pro Football Hall of Fame.

"I'm not one of the great athletes like the men behind me," he said during acceptance remarks in Canton, Ohio. "But I'm thrilled to be standing before them. Many of the men in here were my heroes. To be rubbing shoulders with them, it's beyond my comprehension."

No one before had produced a world champion from expansion birth. Neither had anyone televised the Winter Olympics before Tex did from Squaw Valley in 1960. He was then a CBS-TV sport executive who had left the Los Angeles Rams in 1957 as general manager, disillusioned over wrangling ownership.

His job with the Rams fell to the public relations man he hired years earlier: future NFL commissioner Pete Rozelle. And for a lead announcer for the Winter Games, then and thereafter a television rating hit, Schramm chose a talent from the news department named Walter Cronkite.

Rarely if ever have four more disparate personalities as the Cowboys founding fathers united and coexisted for decades—reclusive Clint Murchison Jr., taciturn Tom Landry, teetotaler head scout Gil Brandt, and the gregarious Schramm. Tex explained how and why their system worked during his 29-year career in Dallas.

"There's one thing you must have in football: one continuous line of authority," he said. "The players have to understand that, as far as they are concerned, Landry is the boss. They have to understand that the only person I will listen to is Landry.

"Secondly, they had to understand that I had that kind of backing from Murchison. He emphasized from the very first that any of his contact with the club would be through me. This is the way it has to be if you are going to have a chance to win.

"If everyone doesn't know that there's a definite line of authority, you have chaos. The players might go to first one person, then another. There's no acceptance of responsibility for (not) winning. It's always someone else's fault. When you have that, you have cliques in your team. Then you don't have anything."

Schramm's contribution to the style and substance of the Cowboys and NFL fills volumes. He conceived the Ring of Honor, the Cowboys Cheerleaders, championed the Cowboys as annual Thanksgiving Day hosts, pioneered computer-aided scouting, and recognized the value of national media exposure by insisting that geographically outbound Dallas join a division with New York, Philadelphia, and Washington.

*The chief architect of the Cowboys over its first three decades, Tex Schramm, here with Tom Landry at groundbreaking ceremonies for the Cowboys new practice facility in 1983, was inducted into the Pro Football Hall of Fame in 1991.*

**All-Time Cowboys Defensive Backs**

1. Mel Renfro
2. Cliff Harris
3. Everson Walls
4. Charlie Waters
5. Darren Woodson
6. Cornell Green
7. Deion Sanders
8. Dennis Thurman
9. Michael Downs
10. Kevin Smith

His work on behalf of the League included negotiating an NFL-AFL merger with Kansas City owner Lamar Hunt, introducing instant replay to aid officials, developing the wild-card playoff system, and a myriad of rule changes while chairman of the Competition Committee from 1966 to 1988.

These decisions made headlines. Others as important didn't.

One was a gender-bending act that predates political correctness. Schramm hired Kay Lang as the Cowboys' original ticket manager. She became the first woman to hold a front-office position in the NFL more than 45 years ago.

Also, at that time Dallas hotels did not welcome black players on visiting teams, and housing for black players with the Cowboys was restricted to the city's southern area. Schramm quietly and effectively helped end those discriminatory practices. He never mentioned it.

Schramm—actual birth name Texas—did something rare for any high-profile executive. His home number and address were listed in the Dallas phone book from the day he came to town. Anyone could call, and did, at any hour, and he answered.

Most players who negotiated contracts with Schramm doubted he had a soft heart. However, in certain cases he did, and it turned to mush. He avoided firing anyone in the front office. Tex had them transferred. If it came to a dismissal, he couldn't pull the plug.

Schramm felt his stint as a sportswriter in Austin, where he earned a bachelor's degree in journalism from the University of Texas, gave him latitude to critique local scribes. Since negative news about the Cowboys was an obvious distortion in his view, he called writers at their homes to complain. His complaints were loud, profane, and then laid aside.

"Tex burns fast, but he forgets easily and regrets quickly," said vice president Al Ward.

Schramm's temper often exploded in the press box where he preferred to watch games instead of a luxury box. Dubious penalties against the Cowboys provoked a roar at officials. "You gutless...!" Tex could be internationally loud, too.

He and the Cowboys were in London when Rozelle phoned with results of the USFL versus NFL lawsuit. The NFL had been found guilty of acting as a monopoly and ordered to pay the measly sum of $1. Schramm began to laugh and howl in ever-increasing volume from his hotel suite. The verdict effectively put the USFL out of business.

Tex told Rozelle he'd make the ultimate sacrifice and give $1 from his pocket. He volunteered with enough force to shatter crystal until a gentle reprimand from his adored wife, Marty, interrupted the filibuster.

"Why don't you open the window so the queen can hear?" she said.

Schramm's voice lost volume, and authority, after Jerry Jones bought the franchise in 1989 and turned him out. He spent one unsatisfactory year as honcho of the NFL's new pro league in Europe but thereafter the pro football world he'd known since the 1940s moved on without him.

Idle time gave Tex time to reflect when he wasn't deep sea fishing out of Key West on his boat, the Key Venture. Reflection always returned his heart and mind to the Cowboys, and to whether others thought he'd done enough to ensure an enduring legacy. A few years before his death in 2004 at 83, over dinner in Key West with a writer friend, he raised that question in a melancholy moment.

"Will they remember?" he asked, softly and mostly to himself.

Schramm should not have worried. All who crossed his path considered him unforgettable.

# Cowboys-Redskins Feud

No one can pinpoint the exact moment when the Cowboys-Redskins rivalry turned mean and nasty, and then got worse.

It would eventually involve personal insults, charge and counter-charge of dirty play, team captains refusing to shake hands at the prekickoff coin flip, a funeral wreath thrown into the opposing locker room, and one coach wishing he could fistfight the other, to name a few rancorous episodes.

The first incident between the teams dates back to a distant December in 1961. Some historians consider it the symbolic genesis of hostility that peaked a decade later. Whatever the true origin, relations between Dallas and Washington soured early over a caper hatched by the Cowboys Chicken Club.

A group of Cowboys fans based in Washington—lobbyist, attorney, heart specialist, and a member of the Cowboys board of directors—formed the CCC. It aimed to tweak Redskins owner George Preston Marshall, who had opposed an expansion franchise in Dallas. And, further, because Marshall fielded the last all-white player roster in the NFL.

This was the plot: slip into the D.C. stadium the night before the Cowboys game and scatter chicken feed on the field. Sneak two crates of 76 live chickens, all white except one that was black, into the stadium on game day. Free them during Marshall's pride, the Christmas halftime show featuring Santa Claus. Rejoice when the black bird in particular, representing an obvious racial slur, took the field to scratch for food and embarrass Marshall.

All went well until minutes before the entrance cue. Alas, a clucking noise from beneath canvas-covered crates in a dugout led to the discovery f the feathered cargo. The CCC had been thwarted and passed into history with a cackle.

A more precise date of the birth of the rivalry would be in 1971 when thumb-licking George Allen was hired to coach the division rival Redskins. Of Allen's extravagant spending habits on players and training facilities, club president Edward Bennett Williams lamented, "I gave him an unlimited budget and he exceeded it."

Allen and the Cowboys already disliked each other, based on an earlier wrangle when Allen headed the Los Angeles Rams. Accusations of spying on practices prior to a Cowboys-Rams game in 1967 arose from the opposing camps.

Tex Schramm told of a suspicious vehicle parked near the Cowboys' practice field. He alleged a license plate check traced the car rental signature to Johnny Sanders, head scout of the Rams. Schramm huffed and lodged an official complaint with NFL commissioner Pete Rozelle.

Allen responded with a hilarious countercharge. He claimed the Rams saw a man sitting in a eucalyptus tree with binoculars, spying on their practice. A futile chase of the culprit ensued. Allen said the man looked like Cowboys scout Frank "Bucko" Kilroy. This was a comical comeback. Kilroy weighed almost 300 pounds and did well to climb out of his shoes, much less shinny up a tree.

The Rams won that '67 game (35–13), and while nothing came of the spy charges, a distrust of Allen settled into the Cowboys psyche. Allen felt less respect for the Cowboys, whom he considered showbiz-slick, arrogant, and unethical.

"Tex and Dallas are always carrying the Holy Grail," he mocked.

Allen's players easily adopted his anti-Dallas campaign. Some even expanded on it.

"If you grew up in the metro Washington area, you grew up a die-hard Redskins fan," declared Washington offensive tackle Jim Lachey. "But if you hated your parents, you grew up a Cowboy fan."

Beating the "goddamn Dallas Cowboys," as he referred to them, became Allen's obsessive target. He scripted a psychological theme during each countdown week to distract the Cowboys and energize the Redskins. Allen once told his players he wished he could travel alone to Dallas on game day. There he'd meet Tom Landry at midfield of Texas Stadium and duke out a winner-take-all result.

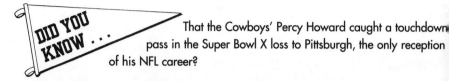

That the Cowboys' Percy Howard caught a touchdown pass in the Super Bowl X loss to Pittsburgh, the only reception of his NFL career?

Allen as a sneaky operator evolved into a source of near paranoia for the Cowboys. For example, the top floors of a motel located behind an end zone overlooked their practice field. The security-conscious Cowboys rented every room with a view and kept them vacant for a week in advance of Allen coming to town.

"Any helicopter that came over, the coaches would look up like, damn that's George Allen up there with a notebook," recalled Walt Garrison.

Mel Renfro's take on the Redskins coach expressed a majority opinion. "He was basically a crook...the Richard Nixon of football," Renfro said.

A philosophical schism also created grudges. The Cowboys were devoted to sustaining future success through the college draft. Allen sneered at that process and boasted, "The future is *now*." He treated the draft with disdain, trading choices for grizzled veterans who became inspired by their Over the Hill Gang nickname. A test of respective systems hung with every outcome.

Yet what truly inflamed the series beyond boil was that both teams for the next nine years ('71–'79) were Super Bowl threats and met twice annually during the regular season. "Any time two contenders continuously play, you will not have friendly football," Lee Roy Jordan remarked. If friendly competition ever existed, it vanished forever in '72 during a 34–24 Dallas victory at Texas Stadium.

Allen accused receiver Lance Alworth of using four illegal crack-back blocks at the knees of his linebacker, Jack Pardee. "Vicious," said Allen, and faulted Landry for allowing a tactic designed to injure. So did Pardee, who said, "That's what comes from the all-righteous Tom Landry, who is holier than thou and all-good."

The Cowboys filed a counterclaim on the same issue. Their linebacker, Chuck Howley, suffered a season-ending wrecked knee when hit by Redskins receiver Charley Taylor. Tempers were still hot when a third game between the teams took place in Washington at the NFC championship game.

Wild card Dallas had advanced via a Roger Staubach–ignited rally that beat San Francisco 30–28. Inactive since a preseason shoulder

*Indicative of the fierce play between the Cowboys and Redskins, Cowboy Harvey Martin puts heat on Washington's Billy Kilmer.*

# TRIVIA

Answers to the trivia questions are on pages 163–164.

> **Who holds the career club record for most blocked extra points, field goals, and punts?**

separation, Staubach replaced Craig Morton and threw two touchdown passes in the last 1:30 to beat the 49ers. Landry named him to start the playoff against the Redskins, who shut him down and almost shut out the Cowboys in a 26–3 rout.

"They just had the wrong man in there...He [Staubach] was rusty and couldn't find his secondary receivers," said defensive tackle Diron Talbert. Staubach never forgot or forgave Talbert for that remark. In years to come, as team captains, they met stiffly at midfield for a coin flip and refused to shake hands.

Staubach became a regular target of Allen's mind-manipulation ploys. He said Staubach "couldn't read defenses." Through Talbert, the Redskins dared Staubach to run, the better to knock him out and leave rookie Clint Longley as a hopeless reserve. Their wish came partially true when Longley replaced an addled Staubach in '74 and beat Washington with a last-second pass to Drew Pearson, 24–23.

Feelings were ruffled for other reasons. The Cowboys yelped that Redskins kicker Mark Moseley got added distance from a shoe loaded with lead. Allen howled that D. D. Lewis, centering on a punt, drew the Redskins offsides with an illegal head bob to keep a winning Dallas drive alive. Joe Theismann's flamboyance annoyed the Cowboys. Washington felt the same about Thomas "Hollywood" Henderson. And so on. Fumes from previous wounds still lingered after Allen's departure from Washington in '77.

Harvey Martin received a funeral wreath falsely inscribed from Washington and threw it into the Redskins locker room following a 35–34 Dallas victory in '79.

Hoax revealed, a chastened Martin sent an apology to the Redskins and Pardee, now the head coach.

Relations slowly cooled in Allen's absence because, as Schramm pointedly reminisced, "What Allen added (to the rivalry) was the Tabasco." Hence a series blissfully inflamed by insult, mutual suspicion, and hostility, receded into history as a diminishing echo.

# The Mad Bomber

No player fell harder, faster, or farther than Clint Longley, whose hero-to-villain career began with fanciful flourish and ended in bizarre disgrace. His story still puzzles and tantalizes 30 years after he vanished from the NFL scene.

Longley arrived in 1974, a rookie quarterback from Abilene Christian College, and quickly emerged as a fascinating figure. He brought a slingshot arm and gunslinger's aptitude to the position. His Wild West persona was enhanced with a background note that he hunted rattlesnakes as a hobby.

Longley had an innocent face that proved deceiving, brown curly hair, cherub cheeks, and the big-tooth smile of a 6'1", 193-pound teenager. There was a carefree air about the way he threw passes and a wayward direction to some of them. One caromed against Tom Landry's coaching tower during training camp to earn Longley his nickname: the Mad Bomber.

Unpredictable and unorthodox, he was maddening to defend.

"He looks one way and throws sidearm in another direction," safety Cliff Harris observed. "In practice, guys pull muscles trying to go where he throws the ball."

Longley stuck as the compatible backup for Roger Staubach, a relationship doomed to deteriorate into two physical clashes between them within the next 24 months. Staubach's career would flower until it reached Pro Football Hall of Fame pinnacle. Longley's saga would end in exile and a reclusive life extending to this day.

Thus the Cowboys began the '74 season with an erratic rookie as their only quarterback insurance. The situation was uneasy, and the season turned shaky enough at 6–5 to keep Staubach taking every snap through the first 11 games. Next loomed a home date against the despised Washington Redskins.

No respectable Cowboys-Redskins game could begin without a pre-kickoff issue involving personal insult, charges of spying and illegal plays, and in general, word that the other side was up to no good. This time Diron Talbert, Washington's salty defensive tackle, added a new item to the spicy menu: a threat that Staubach might not finish the game.

Talbert noted the disparity of experience between Staubach and Longley with an ominous forecast.

"If you knock Staubach out, you've got that rookie facing you. That's one of our goals. If we do that, it's great. He's all they have," he said.

As Talbert predicted, the Redskins kayoed Staubach in the second quarter of the game they led, 16–3. Longley came in with low expectations for a rookie making his NFL debut against a stout 10–4 rival that would tie for the NFC East title. Yet Longley bombed away until he completed 12 of 21 passes for 209 yards and two touchdowns. His game-winning stunner covered 50 yards to Drew Pearson with less than 30 seconds left to beat Washington, 24–23.

"It was a triumph of the uncluttered mind," marveled guard Blaine Nye.

No one knew it but Longley's career had reached its lone peak. He kept a tape of that game and played it during future training camps—only two more with the Cowboys. His lifestyle remained unchanged otherwise.

"I get a few more phone calls, and I get a few more letters. And I get to shower with the veterans. That's about it," Longley said.

# TRIVIA

After Harold Jackson of the L.A. Rams caught four touchdown passes against him, this cornerback said, "If you learn by mistakes I ought to be a genius." Who was he?

*Answers to the trivia questions are on pages 163–164.*

Longley receded into the background during the '75 season, his only action starting for an injured Staubach and winning the finale against the New York Jets, 31–21. Clouds of tension moved in the next spring when the Cowboys signed Danny White, a two-year quarterback starter from the defunct World Football League.

*Clint Longley, replacing the injured Roger Staubach at quarterback, enjoys the limelight after his last-second pass to Drew Pearson beat the Redskins 24–23 in 1974.*

Staubach's theory is that Longley felt threatened by White and a jealous mind-set led to their problems during the '76 training camp. Staubach recalled that Longley turned loner, refused to speak or interact with him and White. He'd also heard that Longley made snide criticism of him personally.

The lid on this boiling kettle blew during a postpractice session when Pearson dropped a Longley pass. Longley made a crude remark directed at the receiver. Staubach heard him and reacted with irritation.

"Clint," he said, "I'm getting tired of you talking behind people's backs. Somebody is gonna knock those Bugs Bunny teeth of yours in."

"Are you going to be the one?" Longley replied.

"Yeah, I'd love to do it," said Staubach.

They agreed to meet on a baseball diamond adjacent to the practice field. Both shed helmets. According to Staubach, Longley swung first without warning and grazed the left side of his head. By the time assistant

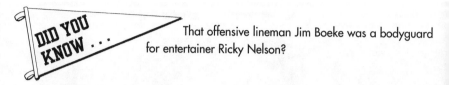

coach Dan Reeves broke up the scuffle, Staubach had Longley pinned beneath him.

Reeves gave Staubach prophetic advice en route to the shower.

"Roger, I'll tell you one thing," said Reeves. "If I were you I'd be careful. I wouldn't turn my back on him."

Staubach's back wasn't turned the next time Longley sucker-punched him. But his head was down, focused on lacing shoulder pads in the locker room when Longley struck. A relaxed target, Staubach fell against a set of scales, bleeding from a cut that required multiple stitches to close. Longley walked to his dorm room, picked up his personal gear, caught a ride to the Los Angeles airport, and was gone.

Evidence confirmed that Longley's assault was premeditated. His luggage had been packed for a getaway. During an earlier lunch with Charlie Waters he'd hinted of a plan that would free him to play elsewhere.

"Clint took his tray, got some ice cream, and rejoined me," Waters recalled. "Then he announced, 'I know how I can get traded!'"

"How?" asked Waters.

"You'll see," said Longley, and then he got up and left.

News that Dallas quarterbacks were duking it out in California, and one of them was straight arrow Staubach, caused a national sensation. At the team's Thousand Oaks home base it created chaos. The switchboard exploded with calls. A fire drill of reporters raced hither and yon in confused circles. No one yet had a grip on the details.

At this jangled moment an overwhelmed Andy Anderson of the public relations staff answered a phone call from Dallas. A radio station had gotten through and a breathless voice rushed to set the scene for his audience.

"This is Radio Station KRLD. We have Andy Anderson on the line with a *live* bulletin from Thousand Oaks. Andy, what can you tell us about the fight between Longley and Staubach?"

To which Andy exclaimed to KRLD's all-live listeners, "I can't talk to you now! I'm up to my ass in alligators out here!"

Staubach has never seen nor spoken to Longley since the day he was blindsided. Nor has Longley publicly addressed why he felt motivated to attack. He wound up attached to San Diego during the '76 season before drifting out of the NFL and into what appears to be desired obscurity.

A Dallas reporter located Longley in the Corpus Christi area and made the last known attempt to interview him in November of 2004. His closest encounter occurred when he trailed Longley on a road that led to the beach. Longley stopped, circled his vehicle, and sped head-on toward the reporter's parked car. He veered aside at the last instant to pass. The one-time hero of yesteryear disappeared in a plume of churned sand.

# Dirty Dozen and Hail Mary

Tex Schramm's vision of a dynasty began to lose focus, blurred, and then disappeared within three years following victory in Super Bowl VI. His projected multiworld champions resembled a Johnny One-Shot winner.

In 1972 they lost the NFC championship game in Washington, 26–3. In '73, they lost at home to Minnesota, 27–10, again with a 10–4 team and at the cusp of qualifying for the Super Bowl. In '74, they skidded to an 8–6 finish and missed postseason for the first time in eight years when the streak included those glorious Playoff Bowls.

Retirements siphoned veteran skill and leadership from the defense that swamped Miami in Super Bowl VI. The careers of Chuck Howley, Bob Lilly, George Andrie, Cornell Green, and Herb Adderley had run their course. Age forced Walt Garrison, Mike Ditka, Dave Manders, and Lance Alworth to hang up offensive cleats.

Bob Hayes left for a cameo season in San Francisco in exchange for a third-round draft choice. John Niland went to Philadelphia. Another trade sent Craig Morton to the New York Giants. Duane Thomas was exiled and successor Calvin Hill departed for Hawaii in the new and soon-extinct World Football League.

Hill's defection was a body blow. He'd been the first Cowboys runner to gain 1,000 yards in a single season. Hill had done it twice with 1,036- and 1,142-yard totals during All-Pro seasons when he also led the team in receiving. His 5,009 career yards ranked second to Don Perkins (6,217) among the club's all-time rushing leaders.

All these absentees left Tom Landry with what, beyond a riddled roster? Perhaps a team also spoiled by success? He wondered.

"Maybe you have to see how it feels to be down before you can come back again," he said prior to the '75 season. "The only value of a season like ours (in '74) comes if the team becomes more determined than it was the year before. We didn't have a losing season, but we were out of the playoffs and out of the money.

"If that means enough to the players, they'll come back."

As seen from the outside, Landry's quandary lay more with physical limitations than soft mental attitude. He lacked enough quality players, according to blunt projections. The Cowboys appeared grounded in mediocrity.

"We were underdogs when the season began," recalled Roger Staubach. "One Dallas paper picked us third in the division. A wire service forecast we'd finish last."

What no one foresaw, including those who wound up on board, was a magic carpet preparing to lift off. Instead of star-crossed, the Cowboys were star-kissed by a series of blessings.

First was Landry's superb staff. It included future NFL coaches Dan Reeves (Denver, NY Giants, Atlanta), No. 6 among all-time winners with 201 victories; Ditka (Chicago, New Orleans), Super Bowl XX leader of the champion Bears; and Gene Stallings (St. Louis, Arizona), who won a national college championship at Alabama. Ernie Stautner, Hall of Fame defensive tackle with Pittsburgh; Jim Myers, former head coach at Iowa State and Texas A&M; and Jerry Tubbs, last of the original Cowboys from 1960 and onetime All-American linebacker at Oklahoma, rounded out Landry's senior aides.

Yet all were dependent on the quality of personnel provided by Gil Brandt's scouting network. Brandt and his bird dogs had gathered many starters-to-be in recent drafts, often through clever trades.

Robert Newhouse arrived in '72 (for Halvor Hagen and Honor Jackson). Golden Richards (for Ron Widby and Ike Thomas), Harvey Martin (for Tom Stincic), and Billy Joe DuPree came aboard in '73. Ed

DID YOU KNOW . . . That Cowboys assistant coach Ernie Stautner was named to the Pittsburgh Steelers 50th anniversary team?

# TRIVIA

Who said, "To me a football game is like a day off. I grew up picking cotton on my daddy's farm and nobody asked for an autograph or put your name in the paper for that."

*Answers to the trivia questions are on pages 163–164.*

"Too Tall" Jones and Danny White were payoffs in '74 (both for Tody Smith and Billy Parks).

No draft surpassed the gusher of '75 that produced 12 rookies on the opening day roster. Randy White (from the Morton trade), Thomas Henderson, Burton Lawless, Bob Breunig, Pat Donovan, Randy Hughes, Mike Hegman, Herb Scott, and Scott Laidlaw were major keepers of the self-named Dirty Dozen. Others of less distinction included Kyle Davis, Rolly Woolsey, and Mitch Hoopes.

"What everyone forgot was that Landry always keeps a sound nucleus of players," said Staubach, referring to veterans Drew Pearson, Cliff Harris, Charlie Waters, Jethro Pugh, Mel Renfro, Ralph Neely, Lee Roy Jordan, and Dave Edwards. Preston Pearson, a 30-year-old tailback waived by Pittsburgh, signed one week before the opener to become "the key to our season," in Landry's analysis.

"They also forgot Tom's abilities as coach," Staubach reminded.

To prove the latter point, Landry revived the shotgun formation he used in the early '60s with Eddie LeBaron and Meredith. An updated version fit scatter-legged Staubach's instinct for operating in space.

"I liked it from the outset," he said. "It shouldn't be a problem for the quarterback to be only five yards deep from the center. I felt comfortable, as if I had more freedom."

The improbable occurred first. Unsung Dallas finished 10–4 to claim a wild card berth. The impossible took longer. That didn't happen until the Cowboys met Minnesota in a divisional playoff. The Vikings were a 12–2 powerhouse, famed on defense as the Purple People Eaters, and sported the NFL's No. 1–ranked passer in Fran Tarkenton.

On December 28, in baseball-configured Metropolitan Stadium, eerie events unfolded involving a piece of fruit, bottle of alcohol, badly aimed kick, the Hail Mary, and a postgame notice of death. The most famous play in Cowboys' history evolved from the weirdest game they ever played.

As Staubach reconstructed it, the Cowboys were once reduced to a hope and his prayer, "Talk about your bleak situations. We were looking at fourth-and-16 from our own 25 with only 44 seconds left. If the Vikings stopped one more play the game would've been over, with us losing 14–10. That was where mini–Hail Mary saved us."

Staubach referred to a 25-yard pass to Drew Pearson, who actually landed out of bounds from the force of Nate Wright's tackle. His gain to the 50 was therefore declared legal. As Pearson lay prostrate on the sideline, a security guard swung his leg with intent to kick him but fortunately missed.

A pass to Preston Pearson failed before Staubach quizzed Drew in the huddle before the next play.

"Remember when you ran the turn and take-off last year against Washington to beat the Redskins?" he said, harking to the Clint Longley connection. Pearson did, but he wondered about Staubach's memory.

"I was thinking, 'How do *you* remember? You were knocked out that game.'"

*Drew Pearson hauls in the Hail Mary pass against Minnesota on December 28, 1975. Vikings Nate Wright (43) and Paul Krause (22) can do little at this point to stop the unthinkable.*

# TRIVIA

When asked about TV evangelists, who said, "How come when they tell you to send your money to Jesus, they give you their address?

Answers to the trivia questions are on pages 163–164.

They agreed on the route. Staubach faded from shotgun formation and pumped left to draw safety Paul Krause away from Pearson. Then he let fly deep to his right where Pearson and Wright jostled for position around the 10-yard line. Suddenly Wright fell, Pearson snagged the ball on his right hip and backed into the end zone from the 5-yard line.

But wait! A flash of color whizzed past Pearson after he made his catch. Was it a penalty flag? Pass interference against Drew since Wright claimed he was pushed? No, it was an orange thrown by some idiot from the stands. At least the fruit was harmless. The next object flung by an angry fan had the potential to injure, and it did.

"There was no deliberate push. I've been asked this question many times," Pearson repeats. "Cowboy fans believe me. Viking fans don't."

To complete the answered prayer—Staubach said he threw and offered a Hail Mary—Pearson threw the football high against the baseball-oriented scoreboard. Hence one game story credited Pearson with the winning touchdown in a titanic 17–14 upset plus a ground rule double.

"I never had a more eerie sensation on a football field than during the aftermath of that touchdown," Staubach said. "The crowd was so shocked there wasn't a sound from the stands. It was as though all of a sudden we were playing in an empty stadium."

Not everyone in the stands was struck dumb. During a TV timeout following the Dallas kickoff, as teams waited resumption of play, the referee suddenly fell where he stood. Blood gushed down his face. He'd been struck in the head by an empty whiskey bottle thrown from seats behind the end zone. Medics led him to the locker room for emergency treatment.

One sad postscript completed the story of the game like no other. Tarkenton's father, a Methodist minister in South Carolina, died while watching the game at home on TV. The bewitched coincidence was that Rev. Tarkenton's first name was Dallas.

# Super Bowl X

En route to a Super Bowl berth that no wild card team had achieved, the road-bound Cowboys needed to beat the touchdown-favored Los Angeles Rams in the NFC championship game. After necessity became reality, the defeated Rams felt it needn't have been done with such emphasis.

Dallas won, 37–7, in a playoff that wasn't as close as the final score indicated. The Cowboys led 7–0, 14–0, 21–0 28–0, 31–0 and 34–0 before the Rams scratched.

"They whipped us in every way," said Rams coach Chuck Knox. "They executed better. They're a great team. I said that at the first of the season and I say that now."

Knox referred to the 1975 season opener in Dallas. There the Cowboys upset his team 18–7 only six weeks after the Rams blistered them in an exhibition 35–7. Also before late-arriving Preston Pearson, the fluid free agent tailback from Pittsburgh, found his niche in the offense.

"Preston is a move man, a tremendous route runner who's like having another wide receiver in the lineup," said coach Tom Landry. "There are few who can do as much with a screen pass as Preston."

Faithful to Landry's description, Preston caught touchdown passes of 15, 18, and 19 yards from Roger Staubach in the Los Angeles playoff. Pearson owned another distinction that illustrated the inbred nature of the Cowboys system. He was the only player who had been active with another NFL team.

Meantime a resilient defense held Los Angeles to 22 yards rushing and 96 passing. Evidence by now confirmed that the Cowboys had found a pass rushing whiz in Harvey Martin, the first Dallas native to appear for the hometown club. Further, that Martin had matured

**DID YOU KNOW . . .** That the Cowboys beat the Detroit Lions 5–0 in a 1970 playoff game, the lowest scoring playoff game in Cowboy history?

enough to recognize people in the franchise it was best to know. Because as a rookie in '73, overeager to assume his end position, Martin ran over a slightly built man on the sideline and snapped, "Can't we keep dudes with no business here away from us?"

The little dude happened to be owner Clint Murchison Jr., who signed Martin's checks.

Qualifying for Super Bowl X in Miami meant a date with the rough-house Pittsburgh Steelers, who'd beaten Minnesota 16–6 in Super Bowl IX. The Cowboys offense in particular appeared overmatched. For example, Blaine Nye drew future Hall of Fame defensive tackle Mean Joe Greene, who bloomed in college at North Texas State in nearby Denton.

An overeducated guard—master's degrees in business and physics and en route to a Ph.D. from Stanford—Nye had a quaint take on his profession. Why did he pursue a career in pro football? "Because playing rugby would have required moving to England," he explained.

Referring to the anonymity of his position Nye said, "I'm like salt. Nobody remembers the brand they buy." His theory of postgame analysis went like this, "It's not whether you win or lose but who gets the blame."

Nye had a pithy reply when probed about competing against Mean Joe in terms equated to the meaning of life. Didn't he feel exhilarated to be tested against the best in a duel of skill, stamina, and manhood?

"No," said Blaine, "I'd rather face a dog any day."

Preston Pearson meantime awaited a prickly reunion with the team that set him adrift five months earlier. Pearson was familiar with Pittsburgh's take-no-prisoner mentality. So was Landry. But they differed on how the Cowboys should react to an opponent that led the NFL in physical intimidation.

"One controversial point Landry emphasized before the game, we were not to allow the Steelers to provoke us into fights," Martin said. "The Steelers *wanted* to fight. Landry felt fighting would take away the concentration we needed, besides which brawling could draw costly penalties.

"Preston thought this advice wrong. He believed if we didn't retaliate against the Steelers' ultrarough tactics, they'd raise the level of violence several notches and pound us to death."

The clash of prekickoff philosophies became a moot point since the game went off as peaceful as a tea party the way liberal officials saw it. Only two penalties for a total of 20 yards were assessed—none against heretofore heavily flagged Pittsburgh. Not even when Steelers linebacker Jack Lambert picked up Cliff Harris and dumped him on his head.

"The Steelers rank as the toughest team I've ever seen, before or since," Martin said years later. "They weren't dirty, but they came close."

In broad strokes, Super Bowl X evolved into a struggle between finesse and force.

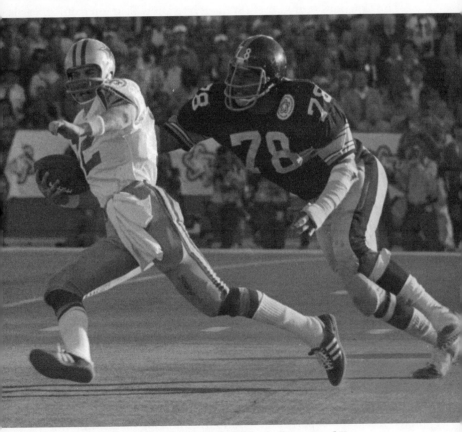

*Roger Staubach eludes the Steelers' Dwight White in Super Bowl X.*

"Our game plan was to shoot the works," Staubach said. "At the time Super Bowl games had a reputation of being conservative and boring. Since we were heavy underdogs we accepted the challenge of taking chances to make things happen."

The Cowboys dared to be different with the opening kickoff when it settled into the lap of ex-Pittsburgh teammate Pearson. Which is what Landry hoped and where he laid a trap.

"Using language you wouldn't hear in a Singapore brothel, the Steelers came thundering down the field intent on decapitating Preston," Martin said. That was Pearson's cue. He slipped the ball to rookie Thomas Henderson on a reverse worth 53 yards before kicker Roy Gerela made a last-man tackle.

The Cowboys scored first (Staubach to Drew Pearson from 29 yards out) and grimly held a 10–7 lead after three quarters. Then force prevailed. Reggie Harrison blocked a Dallas punt out of the end zone for a safety, the Steelers cashed a field goal from the ensuing field position, and Lynn Swann put the game away. Swann, the MVP, caught a 64-yard touchdown pass from Terry Bradshaw for a 21–10 cushion.

Statistics magnified Swann's brilliance—four acrobatic catches worth 161 yards in a performance that sealed his future Hall of Fame induction. Bradshaw's other receivers combined for only 48 yards. Staubach's counter-rally via a TD pass to Percey Howard with 1:48 fell short and left Pittsburgh a 21–17 winner.

An injection of 12 rookies made the future look brighter in '75 than it did in '71 when age began to sap the grizzled Super Bowl VI winners. Recordwise at 9–1 the Cowboys looked even better deep into the '76 season. But beneath that glitzy getaway, unseen termites were at work to weaken the foundation. Staubach was hurt worse than the Cowboys disclosed.

"At midseason I cracked a bone in the little finger of my passing hand," he admitted later. "The next week, against Washington, somebody stepped on the finger and messed it up for good that year. Our running backs, Robert Newhouse and Preston Pearson, were hurt much of the season so the passing game was carrying us.

"Before the injury I was hitting 70 percent passing. Afterward I completed less than 50 percent. I wound up adjusting my passing motion to the pain caused by gripping the ball and developed a sore forearm. We couldn't run and now the passing game failed. Things went to pot at the end of the year."

One thing of special value went to the Rams, a 14–12 first-round playoff victory over the Cowboys, who lost three of their last five games. Staubach was so morose about losing that he overreacted during a post-season meeting with Landry.

"Maybe it's best if you traded me," he told the coach. "I feel like I've let the team down. I don't know if I have them with me anymore."

Landry reacted with characteristic calm, "That's crazy. The team had problems in the running game and you had the injury. You were playing well under the circumstances. We just didn't have support in other areas."

Foremost in Landry's mind was diminishing support from a rushing game that bottomed with 542 yards by Doug Dennison, lowest total for a team leader since 1960. An ace running back could put the Cowboys back on top if they could find one. They did, and he did, which became the story of Super Bowl glory that lay just ahead.

# Hawkeye & Super Bowl XII

There are trades that are good for both teams, better still for one than the other, and best of all for the major figure involved. The Cowboys closed such a deal with Seattle prior to the 1977 draft that altered the course of franchise history and realigned the balance of power in the NFL.

The object of their affection, a difference-making tailback, cost the Cowboys their No. 1 and three No. 2 draft choices. Seattle returned its No. 1 pick, bumping the Cowboys from 14th to second in the draft order. Which meant another player was chosen first *before* Dallas landed Tony Dorsett, four-time All-American, 1976 Heisman Trophy winner at Pittsburgh, and a future Pro Football Hall of Fame inductee.

Few remember it was another runner, Ricky Bell of USC, taken off the top by Tampa Bay.

"We've never had a back with this much breakaway ability," said Landry. "The thing that really impressed me about Dorsett was his tenacity. He might be contained for three quarters, but he would keep after it and break a long one in the fourth quarter."

Scouts touted the breadth of Dorsett's resumé. He was the first in NCAA history to collect three 1,500-yard-plus seasons. He rushed for an NCAA record 6,082 yards, scored 58 touchdowns, and led 12–0 Pittsburgh to the '76 national championship. An ex-Cowboy, Pat Toomay, was further impressed to hear Tony preferred a Dor-SETT pronunciation. The inflection led Toomay to refer to Dorsett as the "French running back."

Dorsett's small stature by pro standards (5'11", 190) raised few red flags, although Tony later said he heard his durability questioned. The

**DID YOU KNOW ...** That Roger Staubach's quarterback rating of 83.4 is best all-time among Dallas signal callers?

...id nicknamed "Hawkeye" for his large, piercing eyes grew up in ...liquippa, Pennsylvania, a tough steel-mill town that also produced ...owboys tight-ends coach Mike Ditka and Oscar-winning musician ...lenry Mancini. As Landry indicated with a compliment to Dorsett's ...enacious nature, the Cowboys had scouted his competitive spirit.

Mutual profit evolved from their professional marriage. The offense ...eceived an injection of its missing ingredient—dazzling backfield ...peed—and elevated the Cowboys to Super Bowl contention. Dorsett's ...lessing was to launch his NFL career with championship caliber ...upport.

Dorsett not only benefited from being united with Roger Staubach, ...ut also the Pearsons (Drew and Preston) and Pro Bowl tight end Billy ...oe DuPree. His entrance coincided with the emergence of the NFC's ...lo. 1–ranked defense.

Harvey Martin produced a spectacular season with a league-leading ...3 quarterback sacks. Victims were described as "Martin-ized." He made ...5 tackles, two fumble recoveries in regular season, two in the NFC ...hampionship game against Minnesota, earned All-Pro recognition, and ...vas named NFL Defensive Player of the Year.

"Harvey is the one I notice," said Washington quarterback Billy ...Kilmer. "He's the stickout who makes big plays for them and gets the rest ...tirred up."

Others alongside Martin didn't go unnoticed. Randy White moved to ...ackle and prospered after a futile two-and-a-half-year trial at linebacker. ...iteady vet Jethro Pugh ("Without a name like Jethro Pugh I might really ...e anonymous") held the other tackle. All 6'9" of Too Tall Jones roamed ...at end. The NFL's best safety duo headlined—kamikaze Cliff Harris and ...erebral Charlie Waters.

Meantime Dorsett's star rose slowly. An early dose of Landry disci-...line made headlines after the rookie overslept a Saturday ...walk-through. Landry told Dorsett he might be benched at Texas ...itadium even though Tony's parents had traveled from Pennsylvania to attend the game. Landry relented slightly by giving Dorsett token carrie in relief of starter Preston Pearson.

Preston continued as starter-in-name until the 10th game whe Landry made Dorsett's first-team status permanent. Teammates by the knew Dorsett was as good or better than advertised.

"Tony makes 10 yards by the time you can blink," marveled Jay Sald

Opponents soon joined the chorus. Dorsett set two club record by scoring on an 84-yard run and rushing for 206 yards agains Philadelphia.

"He's just like he was when they drafted him," said Eagles coach Dic Vermeil. "He's the best in the country."

So were the 12–2 Cowboys who stormed through the playoffs b pounding Chicago (37–7) and Minnesota (23–6), the latter a 12-tackle two forced fumbles, and quarterback sack feast by Too Tall. Dorsett fin ished the regular season with a rookie club record 1,007 yards rushin despite only 21 carries in the first three games. An NFL Offensive Rooki of the Year honor completed his haul of individual awards.

"That man is incredible," Staubach gushed. "I've never seen anyon like him, certainly not in the time I've been in Dallas, anyway."

Stars of the present, future, and past shared the spotlight while th Cowboys were en route to New Orleans to meet Denver in Super Bow XII. Tex Schramm's creation, the Ring of Honor, welcomed a fourth member to the exclusive club at midseason. Six-time All-Pro linebacke Chuck Howley, MVP of Super Bowl V, joined Bob Lilly (1975), Don Meredith, and Don Perkins (both in 1976) on the October day th Cowboys blistered Detroit, 37–0.

"I don't know that I've seen anybody better at linebacker than Howley," said Landry, who issued compliments sparingly. Howley had a serious persona and old-school impatience with youthful indecision. A rookie lineman once asked Howley in practice exactly where Chucl wanted him to line up.

"I don't care. Just stay the hell out of my way," Howley snapped.

*Tony Dorsett, where many of his dazzling runs ended up, in the end zone, scores one in the Cowboys 27–10 win over the Broncos in Super Bowl XII.*

Howley sometimes reacted on instinct rather than the programmed defense. As often as not, he wound up in the right place.

"There's a real irony in my life. When I look back on all the really big plays I've made in my career, I realize I've always been out of position when I made them," he admitted.

Super Bowl XII produced a quarterback oddity in that Denver's starter, Craig Morton, formerly occupied the same status in Dallas.

## TRIVIA

**Who holds the Cowboys record for most yards per carry in a career (500 rushes minimum)?**

*Answers to the trivia questions are on pages 163–164.*

Staubach's superior mobility had been a swing factor in evicting Morton from the Cowboys, and that difference would surface to influence the outcome of their reunion.

The Broncos were 12–2, fielded the NFL's top-ranked defense, and sparked a team color–related Orange Crush mania in Denver. None of it kept the Cowboys from being installed as six-point favorites. Martin agreed with the odds.

"Orange Crush is a soda water, baby, you drink it. It don't win football games," he said.

Here and there a pregame voice thought it would.

"I predict the Broncos will win this one," Howard Cosell misinformed prior to a 27–10 victory by the Cowboys.

Oft-repaired knees left Morton a static pass rush target and the Cowboys defense pounced on his lack of movement. The result was an eight-turnover catastrophe for Denver—four first-half interceptions of Morton and four fumbles. Randy Hughes claimed two fumbles and made a pick; Aaron Kyle, Benny Barnes, and Mark Washington each stole a pass; Bruce Huther, Kyle, and Martin covered the other fumbles.

"I've played some bad games. I certainly played one today," said Morton. "Now we'll prepare to get back in this thing next year."

Staubach was sympathetic to Morton's plight, "If Craig and I had switched sides the Cowboys still would have won. I couldn't have done anything in that situation, either."

Morton had been smothered by relentless pressure from Martin and White, honored as first-time co-MVPs. Other highlights were Butch

Johnson's fingertip catch of a 45-yard touchdown pass from Staubach and fullback-turned-passer Robert Newhouse's 29-yard scoring toss to Golden Richards.

"Overall I think the 1977 team was the best Dallas put on the field while I was active," Staubach said. "The '71 team was close to it and similar—strong running game, good passing game, tough defense.

"Winning a Super Bowl the first time is an unbelievable thrill. There is more maturity about it the second time. One thing it demonstrates is that the first time wasn't an accident."

Thus Dorsett's charmed football life continued. Within the space of 12 months his teams had won a national college title and a Super Bowl. Neither he nor the Cowboys could conceive that their first NFL championship together would be the last.

# Three Little Things

Years earlier the Cowboys brought a mute to the Super Bowl. This time they imported a magpie.

Duane Thomas wouldn't talk before Super Bowl VI. Thomas "Hollywood" Henderson wouldn't shut up prior to Super Bowl XIII in Miami. The former had nothing to say. Henderson didn't know when he'd said enough about the Pittsburgh Steelers.

Hollywood's verbal harpoons made him the interview darling of the media horde, if not all of his teammates. His remarks were so outrageous that he shared the cover of *Newsweek* with quarterback Terry Bradshaw, an immediate target for taunting.

"Bradshaw is so dumb that he couldn't spell *cat* if you spotted him the *c* and the *a*," he said. As for linebacker Jack Lambert, Henderson didn't like him " 'cause he don't have no teeth." Noting that Randy Grossman had replaced the injured starter at tight end, Hollywood sniffed, "How much respect can you have for a backup tight end? I mean, he's the guy who comes in when everyone else is dead."

If the Steelers were inflamed by these insults, they kept it to themselves. The best counterpunch came from an unexpected source, the dust dry persona of Coach Chuck Noll. Referring to Henderson's bombast, Noll curled a lip and said, "Empty barrels make the most noise."

Henderson was a habitual scene-stealer who preferred a solo act. Charlie Waters recalled being eclipsed by Hollywood after his best-ever playoff performance. Waters made two interceptions to set up touchdowns and recovered a fumble in a 28–0 NFC championship game victory over the LA Rams.

*Demonstrative on and off the field, Thomas "Hollywood" Henderson reacts with emotion after stopping the Steelers Larry Anderson in Super Bowl XIII.*

# TRIVIA

Who said, "I've never been beaten. Well, maybe once or twice. But I talk myself out of it before I get off the field"?

*Answers to the trivia questions are on pages 163–164.*

"But what happens?" Waters shrugged. "Thomas returned an interception for our last touchdown with seconds left, dunked over the crossbar and that's all anybody wanted to talk about."

Henderson remembered that Preston Pearson objected to his rant against the Steelers. Roger Staubach had a different take, according to Hollywood's memory.

"You know what, Henderson?" Staubach said. "You've taken the pressure off of us. All we have to do is play. You've absorbed all the pressure. You have opened your big mouth and I love it."

Randy White never spoke of Henderson's antics until well into retirement from the NFL. Yet the clarity of his reminiscence confirmed that he hadn't forgotten.

"I was thinking, how could a guy say that? If that were me, I'd be embarrassed enough to stick my head in sand. I don't care how good you are, you don't make those type of comments. At least not the way I was brought up and the way I was coached," said White.

"You don't make those comments before a Super Bowl game, tiddly-winks, or anything else. You respect your opponent. If you do anything give them compliments before you play. You don't tell them you're going to kick their butt. Just tell them how good they are and then kick their butts.

"That's always been better for me. Thomas didn't see it that way. But then," White grinned, "my picture wasn't on the cover of *Newsweek*, either.

So went a rowdy run-up to the first rematch of Super Bowl teams that dominated the event during the '70s. This was the fifth appearance since 1970 by the Cowboys (V, VI, X, XII, and XIII), and third (IX, X, XIII) but not last for the all-winning Steelers, who were destined to capture XIV and XL as well.

Each team had won two Super Bowls. History awaited the winner of XIII to anoint it as Team of the Decade. What might go wrong to tilt the outcome? Coach Tom Landry had the answer in advance.

"When you have two teams so evenly matched, something could happen to throw the whole thing off for us. Just one little thing," he forecast

Instead, it was three things—a dropped touchdown pass, phantom penalty, and fumbled kickoff return. All were huge and descended upon the Cowboys in the second half with Pittsburgh leading 21–14.

The ghastly series began with Dallas at the Steelers' 10 on third down. Substitutions and the play, a pass to venerable old pro Jackie Smith, arrived late, causing Staubach to call timeout.

During a sideline session with Landry, quarterback and coach discussed making the other tight end, Billy Joe DuPree, the hot receiver. But that play required further subs, and a check with officials confirmed that those already on the field had to remain for at least one snap. So they stuck with the pass to Smith.

"Everything worked beautifully except the pass and catch," Staubach recounted. He meant pocket protection held. Smith appeared alone in the end zone, but slipped or tripped slightly as the chest-high pass bounced from his grasp.

Staubach blamed himself for feathering the ball instead of putting steam on it. His hope was to ease Smith's anguish for dropping the last pass of a career en route to Pro Football Hall of Fame induction. The classy Smith made no excuse.

That not-so-little thing cost the Cowboys four points, the difference between a touchdown and Rafael Septien's field goal, also the final margin in Pittsburgh's 35–31 victory.

A discernible momentum shift was evident when the next disaster visited the Cowboys. They trailed, 21–17, but had snuffed the last two Pittsburgh possessions without yielding a first down. The game turned at this juncture.

Benny Barnes was flagged for pass interference against Lynn Swann, a penalty so errant that NFL commissioner Pete Rozelle later publicly admitted it was bogus. Staubach described the action thusly, "The penalty was called against Barnes for allegedly tripping Swann. I never could figure out how Benny could be running full blast downfield and intentionally trip a receiver *behind* him, which is where Swann was. The whole thing took place near our bench. I was standing there and saw it.

"I thought it was interference on Swann for pushing or something like that. The official right on the play was back judge Pat Knight. He made the first signal, waving his arms back and forth for an incompletion. Then here came a flag from over in the middle of the field.

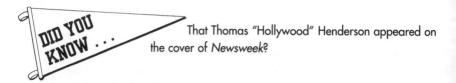

That Thomas "Hollywood" Henderson appeared on the cover of *Newsweek*?

"Incredibly, field judge Fred Swearingen saw the play differently from everybody else in the Orange Bowl. His penalty cost us 33 yards to the 23, and from there Pittsburgh scored for a 28–17 lead."

More misery awaited the Cowboys where even when the Steelers did something wrong, it turned out right. Roy Gerela muffed the subsequent kickoff short and it went into the arms of wedge blocker White. Or rather into a hand cast protecting broken bones. White fumbled at the Dallas 18, the Steelers scored again, and at 35–21 rendered moot a late Staubach rally.

"Boys, you can't say anything bad about this game," Bradshaw told reporters after passing for 291 yards and four touchdowns. Teammate Rocky Bleier said that went for the losing Cowboys, too.

"I give credit to Dallas because they didn't quit. They kept our defense on the field during the fourth quarter. Man, they really gave us a scare," said Bleier.

Defeat cut deep. Perhaps Landry felt it most keenly.

"I'm so upset," he said, "because the game was so special for us. This was the culmination of nine years when we had been to five Super Bowls. We could have been the first team to win three Super Bowls, and it would have been a great climax to an era. But we didn't do it."

Tex Schramm was as downcast but convinced that a return to the Super Bowl remained imminent for his Cowboys.

"It's hell to lose," he said. "But we've been here before, and we'll be back."

Indeed, the Cowboys would appear in more Super Bowls. What would have crushed Schramm to know was that it would be 14 years later, and by then he and Landry would be ousted from the franchise.

# America's Team

A curious thing happened to the Cowboys before the 1979 season began. They were given a new name that complimented their image but complicated the future.

Every spring the team gathered at the practice field for a private screening of the previous season's highlight film. The reel is the work of NFL Films, Inc., which edits, scripts, and provides narration.

Lights dimmed. The projector whirred. Players whooped when they saw the title etched in red, white, and blue.

"Everybody started laughing," Roger Staubach recalled. "We were labeled America's Team and the narrator said something about the Cowboys being 'the Notre Dame of professional football.' I thought it was a joke and they'd bring in the *real* highlight film next."

NFL Films drew the title from crowd scenes of games the Cowboys played around the country. Cameras recorded a large presence of Dallas fans in every stadium in the NFL. The idea of America's Team spun off this display of national allegiance to the Cowboys.

Tex Schramm could have vetoed the title because it was a blatant brag. Schramm instead embraced it since the perception fit his instinct for promoting the Cowboys as distinctive from the herd. Tex reveled at a volley of reaction.

Lewisville High School, north of Dallas, went to the state finals and claimed *it* was America's Team. Others anointed suburban Plano and its long winning history as worthy of the label. Opponents sneered when they beat the Cowboys, as folksy Houston coach Bum Phillips did after a 30–24 win.

"They may be America's team," said Bum. "But I'd rather be Texas' Team."

## All-Time Cowboys Offensive Linemen

1. Larry Allen
2. Rayfield Wright
3. John Niland
4. Nate Newton
5. Pat Donovan
6. Ralph Neely
7. Erik Williams
8. Mark Tuinei
9. Herb Scott
10. Mark Stepnoski

Jack Reynolds of the Los Angeles Rams referred to a hostage crisis overseas by sniping, "Well, if they're America's Team we ought to send them to Iran."

Staubach understood why the name inflamed rivals.

"If I'd been on the other team I'd have given it to us, too," he said. "Every time we lost, somebody on the other team *always* mentioned it. Of course, when we won nobody said anything."

The '79 Cowboys expected to win big. The team that won and lost consecutive Super Bowls was intact—older, wiser, and theoretically better. Before they could prove it, something else happened that was more confounding than curious.

Ed "Too Tall" Jones retired before training camp opened to become a heavyweight boxer. The shock was immense. Another followed when secondary quarterback Charlie Waters suffered season-ending knee damage during an exhibition in Seattle. At the same time, Thomas Henderson's alcohol and drug-fueled rebellion gathered speed toward his November dismissal from the team.

Strung together, those three cases wreaked havoc to the left side of the defense where all were stationed. Since offenses are right-hand oriented, more plays are run in that direction, which is to the left of a defense. The Cowboys missed their strong side end and safety, and play of the linebacker in between them was fading fast.

Those wounds plagued the Cowboys, who had to win four games in the final two minutes to finish as cochampions of the NFC East with an 11–5 record. It took that many Staubach-inspired rallies to offset a staggering 313 points yielded by the defense, 105 more than the year before and the most since the 1963 team leaked 378.

Henderson long had been a disciplinary problem for Tom Landry. He back-talked the coaches, loafed in practice or refused to practice, and dozed through meetings. Landry once discovered Henderson asleep, wearing dark glasses with the lights out during a film review.

"Thomas, can you explain why you have sunglasses on in the dark?" he said, after flipping the lights on.

"Coach," said Henderson, unfazed by being caught napping, "when you are cool, the sun is always shining."

Henderson was done after the Cowboys lost the season's 12th game to bitter rival Washington at RFK Stadium 34–20. He played poorly and spoofed defeat in progress by hamming it up on the sideline, waving a towel at the crowd.

Landry called Henderson to his office and fired him the next morning. As he later admitted, Hollywood appeared with a cocaine-packed nose. In a final show of bravado and resistance to authority, Henderson told Landry he could do no such thing.

"You can't put me on waivers. I quit!" he shouted.

Henderson was out of his mind for the season finale at Texas Stadium between the Cowboys and Redskins. The usual feud was brewing, heated by the NFC East title at stake and by a tack-on field goal Washington coach Jack Pardee ordered with nine seconds left in the first game.

The Cowboys were infuriated over what they saw as a rub-it-in insult. Pardee defended his decision as necessary padding in case a playoff spot hinged on a point-differential tiebreaker. His team's situation was odd—it could lose to Dallas and still make the playoffs if St. Louis lost to Chicago by fewer than 33 points.

"In the tradition of the Dallas-Washington series, it was expected to be a great game but in my opinion it wasn't. It was better than that, absolutely the most thrilling 60 minutes I ever spent on a football field," said Staubach.

The score fluctuated wildly. Washington made the first 17 points, Dallas the next 21, the Redskins added 14 more to lead 34–21 with 6:54

*One of the greatest comebacks in Cowboys history occurred against the Redskins on the last day of the 1979 season. Here Bob Breunig (53) and Benny Barnes (left) slow down Washington's John Riggins before the Cowboys launch their stunning come-from-behind victory, which knocked the Redskins out of the playoffs.*

left to play. Meantime, Chicago covered the 33-point differential, 42–6, meaning the Redskins were playoff road kill if they lost to the Cowboys.

With 2:20 to go, Staubach's 26-yard touchdown pass to Ron Springs made it 34–28. And with 1:46 to go, the Cowboys regained possession thanks to defensive end Larry Cole who dropped John Riggins for a two-yard loss on third down.

"We don't have to rush," said Staubach, bringing calm to the huddle at the Dallas 25. "You gotta believe!" shouted radio analyst Waters, the injured safety turned media expert. A flurry of passes reached the Washington 8-yard line and from there Tony Hill caught the 35–34 winner from Staubach with the clock stopped at 0:39.

"We went from being division champs to the outhouse," said an ashen Pardee, playoff eliminated by the slim margin of four points on a tie-breaker. Other Redskins vented against the Cardinals for their give-up effort against Chicago.

"How can they call themselves professionals?" barked Bob Kuziel. "Did they have a U-Haul backed up to their locker room or what?"

Anger boiled on both sides. Harvey Martin received an unsigned funeral wreath before the game, allegedly from Washington but likely a psyche-up ploy sent locally. Martin threw the wreath into the Redskins somber-enough locker room after the game and

## TRIVIA

**Who were Abdullah Muhammad and Yaqui Meneses?**

*Answers to the trivia questions are on pages 163–164.*

screamed, "Take this s*** back home with you! You're the ones who need it now!"

(Upon Landry's orders, the next day Martin telegraphed apologies to the Redskins team and all the D. C. newspapers.)

Schramm, who had seen every game in Cowboys history, claimed he'd never seen one to match for heroics and theatrics.

"It's the greatest comeback ever," he declared. "It's greater than the '72 playoff because that all happened at the end of the game. We came back twice this time. We had a double chance to cave in."

"This puts Hail Mary in second place," Drew Pearson agreed. Even a Washington aide confirmed this had been a game apart. "If a better football game has been played in the last 10 years I want to hear about it," said Fran O'Connor.

Euphoria had a 14-day shelf life for the Cowboys. They hosted the Los Angeles Rams in a divisional playoff two weeks later and lost 21–19. More key pieces of the Super Bowl roster began to peel away thereafter or were already gone.

Super safety Cliff Harris retired at 31, Rayfield Wright and Mark Washington were let go. Esteemed veterans Jethro Pugh and Ralph Neely had left in recent years. No one knew that Staubach pondered retirement because of an accumulation of concussions dating back to high school.

Staubach's immense skills remained firmly intact in '79. He passed for a career-best 3,586 yards with a 27–11 ratio of touchdowns-to-interceptions at age 37. He was good to go for more seasons.

If he wasn't, he left them laughing because of who caught the last pass of his Hall of Fame-to-be career. A game-ending muddle found the ball nestled in the grasp of startled guard Herb Scott, a thoroughly ineligible receiver.

# An Era Ends

In March of 1980 Roger Staubach went to Tom Landry's office to finalize his retirement. Staubach told Landry in January that there was a 90 percent chance he'd leave the game, a courtesy warning so the coach could plan his roster accordingly.

The breach of their 11-year NFL bond was therefore more of a formality than an unexpected outcome. Landry never directly tried to change Staubach's mind except to say that based on his 1979 performance, Roger could and *should* play another year.

Their parting was formal and sterile, completed without handshake or embrace. Timewise, it consumed roughly one minute for every year Staubach spent with the Cowboys. No overt display of emotion was necessary, Staubach explained.

"That neither of us felt compelled to make this a dramatic good-bye by word or touch simply underlined the depth of our bond. As far as how we felt about each other, a word or handshake was insignificant."

Ever the tease, Staubach was almost out the door when he turned and asked, "Coach, what if I come back next year? Will you let me call the plays?"

Landry caught the humorous intent of surrendering play-calling duty to his quarterback. He replied in kind. "Oh, sure. You can call some from the press box."

Staubach shocked himself when the same question popped out of his mouth. "*Seriously, what if I came back? If I played again would I call plays?*"

Landry's mood remained airy. He smiled and with a soft chuckle said, "No, we have a system going here."

Outsiders often ragged Staubach about Landry calling his plays. Quarterback Fran Tarkenton, who had play-calling freedom at Minnesota, once used that needle only to hear it returned with reference to his 0–3 history in Super Bowls.

"Just think, Fran," Staubach told him during a TV interview prior to Super Bowl XIII, "if Bud Grant were calling your plays, *you* might be here."

Staubach's exit was the entrance cue for Danny White. Son of former Arizona State All-American halfback Wilford "Whizzer" White, he set seven NCAA passing records at the same college. White then started two years for Memphis in the abandoned World Football League, experience that transferred smartly when summoned to sub for an addled or injured Staubach.

His most crucial moment occurred during a '78 divisional playoff. Staubach was knocked out as the first half ended with Atlanta leading 20–13. White rallied the Cowboys to a 27–20 victory that kept alive their march to SB XIII, adding that pelt to two regular-season victories he orchestrated in previous seasons.

"I've worked hard since I've been here just to get myself in position for the opportunity to start," White said. "Now I have that opportunity."

Landry expressed confidence in the success of the team's first new quarterback since 1973.

"White has the experience and background to step and play. He's a smart quarterback who understands our offense. And he has a lot of the same leadership qualities that Roger had," said the coach.

Landry was further buoyed by the return of two excellent veterans missing from a year ago. Lame-kneed Charlie Waters, All-Pro and Pro Bowl strong safety, bounced back in big-game, big-play form. He would tie new free safety partner Dennis Thurman for the team lead with five interceptions.

Too Tall Jones compiled a 6–0 record as a heavyweight boxer but quit the ring anyway to reclaim his defensive end position. Jones never publicly revealed why he left the sweet science.

## TRIVIA

**Who is the only non back or wide receiver to be among the top five in all-time Cowboys scoring?**

*Answers to the trivia questions are on pages 163–164.*

An unnamed source quoted him saying it was because, "I've never been around so many crummy people in all my days."

Teammate Harvey Martin believed Jones revealed the real reason to him. It was technical and related to a shoulder injury Too Tall suffered at Tennessee State. Pragmatic self-analysis told Jones that champions and elite contenders would exploit the resulting flaw in his style.

"I can't throw an overhand right," Jones said. "[Larry] Holmes and [Gerry] Cooney would kill me because of that."

What had boxing been like otherwise?

"Tougher than football," said Too Tall. "You got no pads in the ring."

Another player who never left made a comeback in his 13th and final NFL season. Quiet, football bright Larry "Bubba" Cole emerged from a long snooze to enlarge his legend as the all-time leading scorer in franchise history—among *defensive linemen*.

"He has an instinct you can't coach. Cole moves on the ball in mysterious ways," Landry said after the 16th-round draftee's rookie season in 1968. Landry based his analysis on consecutive game touchdowns Cole

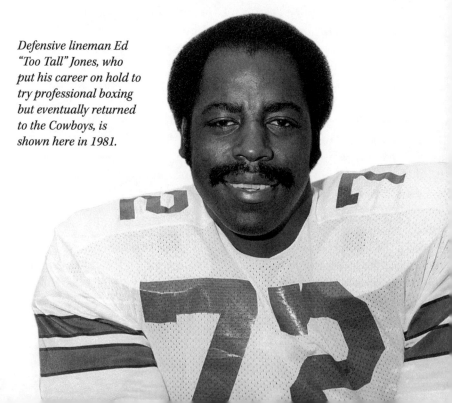

*Defensive lineman Ed "Too Tall" Jones, who put his career on hold to try professional boxing but eventually returned to the Cowboys, is shown here in 1981.*

DID YOU KNOW . . . That quarterback Danny White, who also punted, is the all-time Cowboys leader in total punts and total punt yards?

scored against Washington. He ran five yards with a tipped pass and 21 yards with a recovered fumble.

"I just pick up scraps," Cole shrugged.

Touchdowns are rarities for defensive linemen. Yet after a single season Cole had a 2–1 touchdown lead on Bob Lilly, who played 14 years for the Cowboys. He was two-up on defensive line coach Ernie Stautner, Pro Football Hall of Fame tackle who went scoreless at Pittsburgh over 15 seasons.

And Bubba was just warming up.

Cole made it a three-peat in '69. He rumbled 41 yards with an interception, scoring for the third game in a row against the Redskins. Then a slump set in. Cole didn't score again until he stunned Washington for his fourth and final touchdown via a 43-yard interception runback in Game 12 of the '80 season.

But tell us, Larry. How do you account for a gap of 11 years between touchdowns?

"Anybody can have an off decade," Bubba explained.

Months earlier, the year had begun on a historical note for the 21-year-old franchise. Lilly became the first Cowboy player to be inducted into the Pro Football Hall of Fame. In years to come, Hall of Fame snubs of Bob Hayes, Cliff Harris, Rayfield Wright, and the forgotten Chuck Howley would be the source of controversy in Dallas. [Wright was finally selected in 2006.]

Autumn brought more success, this time on the field for a team that lost its role as favorite in the absence of Staubach.

Yet White guided the Cowboys to a 12–4 record, losing the NFC East title to Philadelphia on a point-differential tiebreaker. His finest hour lay ahead in the playoffs.

The wild card Cowboys beat the Los Angeles Rams in a first-round playoff with a team-record 528 yards in postseason total offense. Tony Dorsett broke Duane Thomas' in-house playoff record of 143 yards by rushing for 160. The oddity of this 34–13 victory was that the Rams nailed Dallas two weeks earlier 38–14. The Cowboys lost by 24 and won by 21—a wild swing of 45 points— against the same team within a span of 14 days.

White's heroics then won the divisional playoff against Atlanta with a Roger-type rally. His two touchdown passes to Drew Pearson in the final 3:40 overturned a 27–17 deficit and beat the Falcons, 30–27. Pearson caught the winner with 0:42 left, and that left his coach gasping.

"It was our third miracle," said Landry, with apparent reference to the Hail Mary pass and 35–34 thriller against Washington the year before. Victory sent the Cowboys to Philadelphia for the NFC championship game. There they were greeted by minus-16-degree wind chill and Coach Dick Vermeil's crocodile tears over his team being "injury ravaged."

Supposedly crippled Wilbert Montgomery ran 42 yards to score on Philadelphia's second play and the Eagles defense did the rest. The Cowboys lost 20–7 but could boast completing their 15th consecutive winning season with a future promising more of the same.

The same didn't mean stalling at the championship game level. But such was their unwelcome, onrushing fate.

# The Catch & The Run

Two plus decades beyond his winless expansion season, Tom Landry had climbed the ladder of all-time winning NFL coaches to rank third behind George Halas of Chicago and Curly Lambeau of Green Bay.

In another sense, he hadn't made any progress.

Landry made that point with a droll reply to a gee-whiz reminder in 1981 that he was the only coach in team history.

"That's one way to look at it," he said. "The other is I haven't had a promotion in 21 years."

If Landry, even in jest, felt his career lacked upward mobility, the Cowboys of '81–'82 knew the reality of bumping their heads against the same ceiling. Defeats in consecutive NFC championship games made it three slips in a row at the lip of the Super Bowl cup, inflicting wounds that festered until losing became epidemic.

Yet there were moments of grandeur before the overcast skies arrived. Highlights involved two of the team's best players and the odd route each traveled to become a Cowboy.

Cornerback/free safety Mel Renfro was the fifth member inducted into the Ring of Honor. Renfro ended his career (1964–1977) awash in honors earned and en route: team career leader in pass interceptions (52) and kickoff returns (26.4 yard average), 10 Pro Bowl and four All-Pro credits, 1971 Pro Bowl MVP and Pro Football Hall of Fame inductee (1996).

Renfro was labeled damaged goods while finishing at Oregon as an All-American halfback and school-record-setting 100-yard sprinter and high hurdler. He slid to the Cowboys as a No. 2, a devalued prospect because of whispers that there was no position that fit a player with one hand. Renfro hurt his right hand smashing it against a mirror in anger over the assassination of President John F. Kennedy.

"I partially cut the medial nerve," Renfro recounted. "The rumor went out that I'd never play football again, that I didn't have use of my hand. That just wasn't true but the rumor persisted and I was passed up on the first round. That scared everybody some more."

Renfro transferred the fright to opposing quarterbacks and set a single season club record of 10 interceptions from safety in '69. His mark stood until broken in '81 by a rookie.

Everson Walls was raised two miles from the Cowboys' old practice field and led the nation in interceptions at Grambling, but he was snubbed in the draft because he was too slow. The free-agent dragnet brought him back home.

*A great moment in NFL history, Dwight Clark hauls in this Joe Montana pass with only seconds remaining to clinch the NFC Championship in 1982. For the Cowboys, however, it was more a day of infamy.* Photo courtesy of Getty Images.

"I took it as a challenge that nobody drafted me," said Walls. "From the first day, I wanted to prove them wrong."

By the fifth game of the season, Walls was starting at left corner. At season's end he'd intercepted an NFL-high 11 passes, broken Renfro's record, and become the first rookie since Lem Barney in 1967 to lead the league in

## TRIVIA

**Who was defensive back Charlie Waters referring to when he said, "He's the guy we all look up to. He's what we'd like to be"?**

*Answers to the trivia questions are on pages 163–164.*

steals. Walls also became only the sixth free agent rookie to make the Pro Bowl where, of course, he intercepted two more passes.

"There isn't a play he can't make," marveled teammate Dennis Thurman.

Walls defended his title in '82 with seven picks to earn more All-Pro and Pro Bowl recognition. Thus he was suddenly the only player to lead the NFL in interceptions his first two seasons; the only Cowboy to lead the league in steals twice; the second player to lead the NFL two years in a row; and with two more steals, the owner of the Pro Bowl career record for interceptions with four.

How ironic that fate chose Walls to be linked with an anguished loss to San Francisco in the '81 NFC championship game at Candlestick Park. Unfair as well, since he made two interceptions and recovered a fumble; the Cowboys leaked a game-winning, 89-yard drive to the 49ers; and the pass that beat Dallas 28–27 may not have been aimed at the receiver who caught it in the end zone.

It was a robust season until that moment. Kicker Rafael Septien tied for the NFL scoring lead with 121 points. Walls won the interception crown. Middle linebacker Bob Breunig topped the team tackle chart for the fifth consecutive year. Tony Dorsett rushed for a club-record 1,646 yards, only 28 short of NFL leader George Rogers of New Orleans. He also became the Cowboys' all-time leading rusher with 6,270 yards, replacing Don Perkins and his 6,217 total.

"Tony is the epitome of an artist," said Jim Brown, famed Cleveland runner and then the NFL's career rushing leader. "No small back in football can touch him."

The run-up to the playoffs went smoothly. A 12–4 record won the NFC East title by two games over Philadelphia. A 38–0 thrashing of

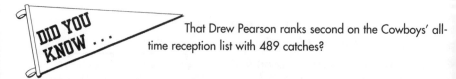

That Drew Pearson ranks second on the Cowboys' all-time reception list with 489 catches?

Tampa Bay sent the Cowboys to California in high gear. However, back in October there'd been a warning tremor at Candlestick.

The 49ers beat Dallas 45–14 to reverse by 76 points their 59–14 loss in Texas Stadium 12 months earlier. San Francisco now had a different quarterback named Joe Montana.

So it was Montana, behind 27–21 with 4:54 left and already intercepted three times, whose legend expanded as he led a game-winning, 13-play march. The 13th snap, on third down from the Dallas six, evolved into an impromptu jackpot.

Montana rolled right until nearly out of bounds. He left his feet to pass over the upraised arms of a leaping Too Tall Jones. Elevated to clear 6'9" Jones, his pass appeared headed high beyond the back line of the end zone. But out of nowhere and seemingly catapulted by a trampoline, 6'4" Dwight Clark rose above a flurry of scrambling players.

Clark gained the altitude of a 747 to make The Catch with the clock drained to 0:51. Whatever the coverage, it vanished during the jailbreak blur of uniforms. Watching helplessly, the nearest defender to Clark turned out to be Walls.

Drew Pearson months later applied a tantalizing postscript. He said he met Montana and his wife at a card-signing show, and he claimed that the quarterback confessed his true intention on the pass Clark caught.

"To paraphrase Joe, he said he was just trying to get rid of the ball," Pearson recalled. "Maybe he was saying that to pacify me."

Of course, by then it didn't matter what Montana said or meant. It was what he'd done to the Cowboys.

Their '82 season ended on the same deflating note despite setting an NFL record so oddly brilliant it can never be surpassed. To happen, the Cowboys needed to be jammed against their 1-yard line in Minnesota. This was done when Timmy Newsome muffed a kickoff and like a farmer shooing chickens, chased it out of bounds there.

Amid sideline confusion, fullback Ron Springs failed to join the first-down huddle. Dorsett assumed his position for a handoff and burst up the middle to score from a never-done-before distance of 99 yards. And with *only 10 men on offense!*

Elsewhere, a strike shortened the season from 16 to nine games and produced a 6–3 finish. Landry won his 200th regular season game against Washington. Finally, events during a 31–17 loss in the NFC championship game at RFK Stadium created a quarterback ruckus that would depose Danny White as the starter.

The sequence began when White was knocked out late in the first half with the Cowboys behind 14–3. Understudy Gary Hogeboom led two touchdown drives in the third quarter to bring Dallas close at 21–17, then offered a preview of his ingrained pattern of inconsistency. Hogeboom threw two interceptions to donate Washington's last 10 points.

"The quarterback position will be very competitive with us now because of Gary's emergence against Washington," Landry predicted. He was right about high stakes competition, but if he thought it would produce better results, the coach was wrong.

# Decline

The Cowboys kept winning and qualifying for playoffs during the next three years, but the 1983–1985 seasons marked a departure in terms of the volume of victories and postseason success.

The Cowboys won, not as much as before, but enough to extend their NFL record of 20 consecutive winning seasons dating back to 1966. In professional sports history, only the MLB New York Yankees, and the NHL Montreal Canadiens and Boston Bruins had longer winning streaks.

The Cowboys went to the playoffs, but not as often, and each time it was a brief in-and-out experience. In '84 they failed to go for the first time in 10 years and only the second time in 19 years. The slide toward mediocrity and worse had begun.

Their fate eventually would mirror the posture of Charlie Waters when he closed his splendid NFL career in the '81 NFC championship game at Candlestick Park. Dwight Clark won it for San Francisco in the final minute with The Catch from Joe Montana, 28–27.

When Clark scored his six-yard touchdown, Waters dropped to his knees in anguish and fell face forward into muck. So much pregame rain had fallen that the NFL abandoned resodding the field. Instead tons of small moisture-absorbing pellets were spread on the surface and spray-painted green.

"When my face mask hit the ground it didn't provide any protection from the mush," he said. "I managed to push myself back up to my knees and had the presence of mind to capture both the gravity and irony of the moment.

"Well, perfect," I thought to myself. "Instead of MVP in the Super Bowl, here I am ending my career with my face buried in green kitty litter."

## All-Time Cowboys Receivers

1. Michael Irvin
2. Bob Hayes
3. Drew Pearson
4. Tony Hill
5. Jay Novacek
6. Frank Clarke
7. Doug Cosbie
8. Alvin Harper
9. Billy Joe DuPree
10. Jason Witten

This three-year slice of Cowboys history consisted of a series of deceptions. In '83 the team appeared as strong as ever with its late-season 12–4 record. In '84 Gary Hogeboom loomed as quarterback of the future. In '85, as improbable NFC East champions, the Cowboys were rebounding.

All of this hid the team's decay.

Danny White withstood Hogeboom's challenge in '83 to produce a still-standing, single-season, team-scoring record of 479 points. The Cowboys scored 30 or more points in nine games. So what went wrong later?

In one memorable instance, it was White's gambling spirit. It served him well when he ran for first downs 15 out of 19 times from punt formation. But not this time, when coach Tom Landry told him to attempt a hard count to draw Washington offside on fourth down.

"I promised him I wouldn't snap the ball," White recalled. "But I saw they had a punt return unit on. So I yelled a line audible, nobody believed it, and they stuffed us. All the while Landry is jumping up and down hollering, 'No, Danny, no!'"

The Cowboys lost that game 31–10. They lost the next at San Francisco, 42–17, to finish 12–4. Then they lost their third in a row, a playoff to the Los Angeles Rams at home, 24–17, and Landry fixed '84 plans around Hogeboom.

Another significant change was the sale of the franchise in May from the Murchison family to Dallas businessman H. R. "Bum" Bright and an

11-member limited partnership. The terminal illness of Clint Murchison Jr. forced the transfer, and Landry would miss the original owner's abiding loyalty. Bright would eventually issue a stinging public rebuke of Landry, whose relationship with the new owner was frosty from the onset.

Landry's uncertainty over dumping White for Hogeboom helped prompt his famous mangle of saying he'd decided, "to go with (Phil) Pozderac," an offensive tackle. The Hogeboom experiment lasted 10 games and produced a 6–4 record and an imbalanced 7–14 ratio of touchdown passes to interceptions.

White completed a 9–7 season in which the Cowboys scored 171 fewer points than the year before and fell from the playoffs. A Silver Season celebration of the franchise's 25th anniversary briefly lifted the gloom when former stars returned for a halftime reunion at Texas

*Danny White, here against Tampa Bay in 1980, replaced the legendary Roger Staubach at quarterback and enjoyed his share of success.*

Stadium. Roger Staubach's induction into the Pro Football Hall of Fame as a first-year eligible also reminded them of better days.

One constant source of levity was always available at Valley Ranch. It was known as The List, country-western song titles and phrases compiled by public relations director Doug Todd. The themes often referred to broken hearts, dreams, and romances.

Only in retrospect would 1985 reveal itself as a watershed campaign that signaled the beginning of the end of the Landry era. Most of the internal tension it produced would not be exposed until the next decade. Beneath the accepted glitter of a 10–6 comeback to claim the team's 13th division title in 20 years stood the brooding figure of president/general manager Tex Schramm. Reality told him miraculous success was a mirage.

Before he could act, the Cowboys yo-yoed through high peaks that fed into a deeper abyss. They extended one streak of consecutive winning seasons to 20. Another ended when former aide Mike Ditka brought Super Bowl champion-to-be Chicago to Texas Stadium. The Cowboys were shut out for the first time in 218 games and absorbed the most lopsided loss in their history, 44–0.

A nondescript 7–9 Cincinnati team applied a 50–24 hickey three weeks later. Defeats of such huge dimensions confirmed deep flaws, yet the Cowboys kept getting up off the floor. They even set an existing team record for quarterback traps (62) with Too Tall Jones (13), Jim Jeffcoat (12), and Randy White (10½) leading the charge. Everson Walls stole nine passes to become the first three-time interception leader in the NFL's 68-year history.

Twin Tonys had terrific seasons. Hill caught 74 passes for 1,113 yards. Dorsett gained 1,307 yards to claim sixth place on the NFL's all-time rushing chart with a career total of 10,832. In and out with injuries, Danny White and reliever Hogeboom combined to pass for a still-intact team record 4,236 yards.

"It was fun coaching the '85 team," Landry reflected. "It was fun watching them get through the peaks and valleys. It was fun watching players reach greater heights than they expected to reach."

But it was no fun when the Cowboys traveled to meet the L.A. Rams in a first-round playoff. Eric Dickerson ran halfway to San Diego while rushing for an NFL playoff record 248 yards. L.A.'s 20–0 victory left Schramm rigid with postgame anger. For the only occasion in their long

# TRIVIA

Who was the first Cowboys
assistant coach to win a
Super Bowl as head coach
of another team?

*Answers to the trivia questions are on pages 163–164.*

association, he pointed a public finger at Landry and his staff.

"When the teacher doesn't teach, the students don't learn," Schramm snapped. According to Schramm, Landry told him at season's end that he was nearing retirement and Schramm needed to prepare a successor. Hence Schramm made a rare intrusion onto Landry's turf by ordering a staff shakeup that might bring his potential heir on board.

He directed the coach to hire Paul Hackett from the 49ers as Landry's key offensive assistant. Schramm's order became so transparent it was reported locally that Landry "didn't know Paul Hackett from Paul Bunyan."

A stranger in his midst was the least of Landry's mounting problems. They began to close around him as he approached his final three seasons with the Cowboys.

# Hard Times

Herschel Walker brought dynamic speed and power to the Cowboys in 1986, but his arrival also served as a distraction. His presence promoted an illusion that the team's downward drift had halted at a shallow depth.

The Cowboys instead slid into a bottomless pit that wrote *finis* to the Landry Era. A period of trial and scorn awaited Tom Landry, who would be insulted by his owner, a rival coach, and then fired three years later.

Walker's coming made huge headlines with visions of a Dream Team backfield alongside Tony Dorsett. He'd been All-Everything wherever he played: NCAA record-setter at national champion Georgia, 1982 Heisman Trophy winner, three-time All-American, and pro mega-star of the New Jersey Generals of the United States Football League.

The rights to sign Walker cost a mere fifth round draft choice in 1985 while the USFL played its third and final season. Analysts lost the scent of the source of decay by comparing this future pick with those that once produced Roger Staubach and Bob Hayes. It's true that the Cowboys made an outrageous steal, but one big-deal success failed to offset too many other personnel failures.

Like a hidden disease, a virus within the system had reduced the talent level for the past decade through poor drafts. There were a few late-round keepers such as Dennis Thurman, Doug Cosbie, Ron Springs, Eugene Lockhart, and Kevin Gogan. But they were too few to sustain a playoff contender.

The fault lay above, in the picking order. Of nine No. 1 draftees from 1978 to 1987, only Jim Jeffcoat made an impact. Injury and derelict evaluation made short careers of the others: Larry Bethea, Robert Shaw, Howard Richards, Rod Hill, Billy Cannon, Kevin Brooks, Mike Sherrard, and Danny Noonan.

DID YOU KNOW ...

That Michael Irvin holds nearly every important receiving record in Cowboys' history, including most catches, total pass catching yards, and touchdowns?

If one incident turned erosion into an avalanche, it happened to Danny White at midseason in New York. The Cowboys were in good shape at 6–2 when a sack by Carl Banks of the Giants broke White's right wrist. It was a free fall from there behind overmatched, second-year backup Steve Pelluer; a 7–9 record snapped 20 consecutive winning seasons.

"That was a terrible stretch we had in the second half of last year," Landry said, referring to a 1–7 finish. "We've never had a stretch like that before in 27 years.

"We've been knocked down before and come back, but we've never been on the skids like last year. And that is bad. That really is bad. The toughest thing we are going to have to do is regain confidence....There is no easy way out of this thing."

There was no escape from glum headlines in 1987.

Clint Murchison Jr. died in March. White's wrist never mended properly. Neither did he achieve the career ambition he outlined: "Until I'm able to put a Super Bowl ring on everyone's finger, there's no way I can be satisfied."

Now the No. 4 all-time NFL rusher with 11, 580 yards, Dorsett began his final year in Dallas upset by a diminished role caused by Walker's entrance.

Meanwhile, the Cowboys announced that Landry had signed a three-year contract, news greeted by the sound of disgruntled fans clapping with one hand. Their hopeful speculation that Landry might retire withered. Unknown until years later, Tex Schramm faced intense pressure from owner Bum Bright to fire Landry.

"I signed that contract because I thought it would take three years to get this thing turned around," Landry said. "We are a very inexperienced team. You don't gain experience overnight. We are in a rebuilding phase, but given enough time can get it done. I don't want to leave the Cowboys when the team is down."

Then the players went on strike two games into the regular season. Game 3 was canceled. Games 4 through 6 went off with replacement players signed from bus stops and checkout counters. The Cowboys were aggressive in fielding the best team possible, and either through pressure from management or by personal choice, veterans (Danny and Randy White, Dorsett) crossed picket lines.

Their presence during a 41–22 replacement-player victory over Philadelphia led to a wicked reprisal when regulars met at strike's end two weeks later at Veterans Stadium. Or so went speculation over why Eagles' coach Buddy Ryan humiliated the Cowboys and Landry in particular.

Ahead 30–20 in the fading seconds, Ryan ordered Randall Cunningham to drop to his knee as if to allow time to expire, but then rise and throw a long pass against the unfocused, beaten Cowboys. This he did, leading to an in-your-face touchdown and final 37–20 score.

"He'll have to live with himself," a pale, stunned Landry said. Ryan lived well long enough to torment Landry's successor and close his Philly career with an 8–2 record against Dallas.

*Heisman Trophy winner Hershel Walker, here in action against the Cardinals in 1987, is seventh on the all-time Cowboys rushing list.*

By the
NUMBERS

**1**—Times Tom Landry was named to the Pro Bowl as a player, 1954

**5**—NFC titles won by Tom Landry

**4–3**—Defensive alignment Tom Landry invented

**6**—Years Tom Landry played in the NFL with the New York Giants

**10**—Years Tom Landry's contract was extended in 1964, after four consecutive losing seasons

**13**—NFC East titles won by Tom Landry

**20**—Consecutive winning seasons in the NFL for Tom Landry, a league record that still stands

**29**—Years Tom Landry coached the Cowboys

**270**—Total games won in the NFL by Tom Landry

**1990**—Year Tom Landry was inducted into the Pro Football Hall of Fame

The season fluttered to a 7–8 conclusion. Walker starred, rushing for 178 yards in his first start and setting an NFL record for the longest overtime run (60 yards) to beat New England, 23–17. An ominous turnstile count closed a show fewer wanted to pay to see. Attendance for the final home game against St. Louis topped out at 36,788, the smallest in more than 20 years. The last comparable crowd was the 35,271 that turned out in the Cotton Bowl for Pittsburgh in 1964. Overall attendance fell 16 percent in 1987 to an average of 49,201.

Nineteen eighty-eight began Landry's long, bleak slog toward the finish line of his 29th and final season. His lone highlight was tying Curly Lambeau of Green Bay for the longest coaching tenure with one NFL team. There wasn't anyone left to coach other than Walker, who gained 1,514 yards.

Free agent Dorsett joined Denver coach Dan Reeves, the former Cowboys assistant, having rushed for 12,036 yards and scored 72 touchdowns for the Cowboys. Tony Hill retired a year earlier as the leading yardage gainer (7,988) among receivers. The last season dawned for Hall of Fame–bound Randy White, Doug Cosbie, Michael Downs, Everson Walls, Danny White, and the latter's one-time successor as quarterback of the future, Steve Pelluer.

The Cowboys were old, slow, and irrelevant. Their owner was also less prosperous. Recession reduced the value of Bum Bright's investments in oil, real estate, and banking to the point that he sought to sell the franchise. The team mirrored Bright's depressed finances en route to a 3–13 collapse and fewest victories since the 1960 expansion year. The swoon included a 10-game losing streak, second only to 12 in a row lost in 1960.

Bright was no source of comfort during hard times. Landry caught the brunt of an infamous public flare-up where Bright declared he was "horrified" at some of the plays the coach called. "It doesn't seem like we've got anybody in charge that knows what they're doing, other than Tex," Bright complained.

Landry made a fitting exit in terms of his 270th overall NFL victory on the next to last Sunday of the season. He beat ever-despised Washington with a lineup that lost 10 straight and eliminated the Redskins from the playoffs, 24–17.

Further review revealed another semihistoric note. A rookie receiver, the first No. 1 draft choice in a decade to make good, caught touchdown passes of 24, 61, and 12 yards and totaled 149 yards on six receptions. His name was Michael Irvin.

Less than three months later, Jimmy Johnson was named the coach of the Cowboys.

# Saturday-Night Massacre

The February 25, 1989, edition of *The Dallas Morning News* displayed a page one picture of two men smiling at each other across the table of a local restaurant. That picture would be worth thousands of words written and spoken before the day ended.

Few would be complimentary.

The men were Arkansas oil man Jerry Jones and University of Miami coach Jimmy Johnson. The restaurant was Mia's, featuring Tex-Mex style food. Jones and Johnson had chosen one of Tom Landry's favorite places to eat. There they sat—the night *before* Jones fired Landry as coach of the Cowboys, and Johnson was announced as his successor.

"At least Landry wasn't there that night. He was the only element missing from a complete fiasco," recalled Johnson, who had pleaded with Jones to stay out of sight and order hotel room service.

The picture required neither translation nor interpretation. It shouted that ownership of the Cowboys had changed hands. But the buyer wasn't anyone who sniffed around and kicked the tires during weeks of speculation that Bum Bright was serious about selling. It was this stranger from the Ozarks.

Worse, of course, the restaurant scene meant Landry was out but left dangling until informed in person. Jones and tearful Tex Schramm assumed that duty later the next day when they flew to meet Landry at his resort home near Austin.

"You've taken my team away from me," Landry was quoted as telling Jones.

A press conference to announce the sale took place that evening at Valley Ranch. Jones faced an overflow, hostile audience. Johnson meanwhile

That Tom Landry was paid only $34,000 to coach the Cowboys in 1960?

returned to Miami, putting distance between him and the public relations debacle in progress.

Like all else written on the occasion, savage reaction from one local columnist flayed Johnson for his absence:

"Johnson's first trophy is the Bad Taste Award. What was he doing in Dallas the last few days? Why didn't he stay out of sight until the last minute?

"Johnson's local presence confirmed the worst. He had acted the proverbial vulture perched on a high wire, waiting for the body to quit twitching. Johnson flew back to Miami prior to the Saturday Night Massacre at Valley Ranch. Jones said he and Johnson decided it would be 'inappropriate' for the latter to appear at the news briefing.

"You wonder why. Johnson already had danced around the edges of Landry's wake. Why miss the funeral?"

Another Dallas scribe oozed venom. "As soon as he [Johnson] was discovered, he scurried for cover like a cockroach when the kitchen lights go on," he wrote.

National reviews were uniformly negative. "Jimmy Johnson, by all accounts, isn't a humble man," wrote Jim Murray of the *Los Angeles Times*. "He can't be. He just stood there while they fired America's Coach and gave him his team. It's as if the rustlers just shot John Wayne. I guess we'll all have to get another team."

*The Philadelphia Inquirer* columnist Bill Lyon made this point, "Jones has replaced Landry with Jimmy Johnson. Right off the top, that's a bad trade-off. The Cowboys have taken a precipitous plunge in class. Presumably Jones thinks Johnson can run up the score in the NFL like he has in Miami. The suspicion is that they are both in for a comeuppance."

Even Philadelphia Eagles coach Buddy Ryan piped up to belittle Johnson's college background. "Tell him that there won't be any East Carolinas on his [NFL] schedule," Ryan needled.

Unschooled in media relations, Jones caught volumes of flak and fire for using awkward words and phrases. His take-charge boast at the press conference drew ridicule on top of rebuke for mangling Landry's dismissal.

"We must win. We will win. Winning is the name of the game," pronounced Jones, and added, "we're going to win this year."

An audience that had seen the Cowboys win their way to five Super Bowls yawned at the new owner's obligatory and redundant pledge. Grammar students winced when he used a word that didn't exist—"uncomfortableness"—in a tangled sentence.

Nicknames sprouted on the spot. Jones became Arkansas Crude. Or else he was hillbilly Jethro Jones. Boss Hog also contended for satirical honors. Johnson and Jones would have their identical initials merged into a unit known as The Jaybirds.

Jones caught grief from all directions during and after his debut as owner. One active player felt free to pile on.

"Jed Clampett is the only other oilman I know, and he would have given a better interview than Jerry Jones," said linebacker Jeff Rohrer.

Smirks flooded the auditorium where Jones stood behind a podium and promised to be involved with every aspect of the franchise "from socks to jocks." Few reckoned how seriously he would embrace that mandate in years ahead. There was no doubt that night what it meant to Schramm.

Schramm had joined Jones, Bright, and minority-owner/partner Ed Smith Jr., of Houston, on the stage. He stood to the rear and to the side with his back against the wall. Both hands were dug deep in his pants pockets. It was the pose of a man who knew the verdict before the one-man jury made it official.

A reporter finally noticed Schramm. He asked Jones where Tex fit in all of this.

"Well," said Jones, glancing at Schramm over his right shoulder, "he's standing behind me right now."

Schramm's fate was sealed. Gil Brandt was a goner. The Old Gang's 29-year partnership had been dissolved. The purge soon spread to oust assistant coaches, scouts, and P. R. staff.

## TRIVIA

Tom Landry was a defensive back and punter for the New York Giants and one other professional football team. Which one?

*Answers to the trivia questions are on pages 163–164.*

*Tom Landry, here being carried off by his players after Dallas' win in Super Bowl VI, ended up third on the all-time win list.*

Jones reportedly paid $140 million for the team and Texas Stadium Corporation, almost twice the total price paid by Bright five years earlier. It was also $139.4 million more than the tab Murchison covered to buy the 1960 expansion franchise.

Johnson examined the playing talent Jones bought and blanched. He analyzed it below his 1987 Miami team that won the national championship.

"I was disappointed," Johnson said. "I'd always held the Cowboys in such high regard, almost on a pedestal. I was a little dismayed at what I saw on the field. I'd just come from a team that had more talent."

Was it *that* bad?

"The talent level was not only marginal," he said, "it was below what the rest of the league was playing with."

There was such a helter-skelter pace to the JJ partnership that early on they forgot an elementary item. Two months into the takeover, neither had bothered to negotiate Johnson's contract. According to his memoir, *Turning the Thing Around,* Johnson said Jones came to his office and settled his contract this way, "How long do you want to make it for?"

"I don't care."

"What? Five years? Ten years?"

"I don't care."

"Let's make it 10 years."

"Okay."

Meanwhile a public whose majority called for Landry's ousting flipped to embrace the former coach. A downtown parade was held to honor Landry and approximately 50,000 people cheered his route. It was one of those weird scenes that only occur in conjunction with the Cowboys.

Where else would so many citizens applaud a fired coach whose last team finished 3–13?

# What If...?

Long hidden like the Dead Sea Scrolls, unknown events that influenced the history of the Cowboys were still being discovered after they lay buried for years.

History in this instance involved the search for a successor to coach Tom Landry long before Jerry Jones decided that issue in February of 1989. In fact, the search was set in motion by Landry, who proposed the idea of his imminent retirement to president/general manager Tex Schramm following the 1985 season.

Only Tom and Tex knew that Landry planned to step aside soon or that Schramm didn't try to talk him out of leaving. Landry's warning of his departure was a courtesy so that Schramm could prepare a smooth transition. Schramm was shocked when Landry later made Tex responsible.

While Schramm hunted a replacement:

- Schramm spurned a huge financial bribe to fire Landry.
- One potential successor, who came as close to being hired as to house-hunt in Dallas, later coached the Washington Redskins.
- The top name on Schramm's list of prospects wound up replacing Landry anyway.

All was set in motion when the Cowboys were playoff-humiliated after stealing the '85 NFC East title. Eric Dickerson of the Los Angeles Rams rushed for an NFL postseason record 248 yards during a 20–0 rout. Schramm reacted with fury and disgust in the postgame locker room.

"If the teacher doesn't teach, the students don't learn," he barked, a rare public critique of Landry and his staff.

DID YOU KNOW ... That Tex Schramm developed the sudden death overtime for breaking ties and was instrumental in bringing instant replay to the NFL?

Schramm reprised these scenes in the autumn of 2001 less than 18 months before his death in July of 2003. He had never spoken of them previously.

"I knew it was over at the end of '85," he said, referring to Cowboys' dominance. "I told Landry that. He should make changes. The clock had run out."

This was when Schramm directed Landry to hire San Francisco assistant Paul Hackett as his chief offensive aide. Hackett accepted, with Schramm's pledge that when Landry left he'd be considered for the head coach position.

Schramm talked to other prospects, among them an NFL head coach between jobs. He flew to Dallas for an interview. Schramm drove him to Valley Ranch to scout suitable housing and laid out firm terms.

"I said if he came, he'd come as assistant head coach or a coordinator. With Tom going to leave, I'd make a commitment to him to take Tom's place."

Schramm's bid came in low. His prospect got a better offer as Kansas City head coach. The man Schramm admired during their tenure on the NFL Competition Committee continued his pro career elsewhere and years later, Marty Schottenheimer turned up coaching Washington in 2001.

"I thought Tom would do it [retire] after '87," Schramm said. "The letters I was getting contained terrible reaction to Tom. All of them wanted to get rid of him."

The most cutting reaction came from owner Bum Bright and his "horrified" reaction to Landry's play-calling. Schramm disclosed that Bright dangled the reward of a large green carrot if he would fire Landry.

"I could have made myself a nice pension," Tex recalled. "Bright would've given me anything to do that. He'd have given me Landry's salary, which was considerable, and double mine."

Landry's dawdle over setting a retirement date became a topic of intense media speculation. He was asked about it constantly, but not until a press conference in '88 did Landry deliver a stunning answer.

Landry said he preferred to keep coaching "as long as Tex wants me." Schramm would have been floored if he hadn't been leaning against a nearby wall. The subliminal text wasn't that hard to read. If there was an onus attached to firing Landry, it was on Tex.

Although Landry was failing on the job, Tex couldn't put his finger on the exit trigger.

"I knew it should be done," he said. "I've wondered if a stronger person would have done it. The only reason I didn't is that we started together and I felt a loyalty to him.

"I didn't, and it's probably better off than if I did. I don't know how I'd be looked upon if I did. I'd been Jerry Jones. I didn't want to be Jerry Jones."

Schramm shared his emotions about Landry with Jimmy Johnson, who was twice contacted in '88 about coaching jobs with the Cowboys. Gil Brandt called first about interest in becoming defensive

*Owner Jerry Jones (left) and head coach Jimmy Johnson, holding the Lombardi Trophy after winning Super Bowl XXVIII, proved a winning if combustible combination.*

# TRIVIA

**What TV sports staple did Tex Schramm originate?**

*Answers to the trivia questions are on pages 163–164.*

coordinator, with the understanding of replacing Landry when he left. Johnson said no thanks.

Schramm made the next call when he heard rumors that the Philadelphia Eagles were hot to replace Buddy Ryan with Johnson. The University of Miami coach was now Schramm's top prospect, especially since he'd said Dallas was his dream job. But as Johnson remembered, there was a problem that wouldn't go away. "Tex phoned and asked if I'd be interested in the Dallas job if Landry were gone. The insurmountable obstacle was that Tex absolutely did not want to be the one to tell Landry it was over. Tex wanted to do something, but he didn't know how to get it done. So the issue was closed."

Several coincidences preceded Johnson's hiring on February 25, 1989. In January of '89, when the Super Bowl was played in Miami, he was a guest in the Cowboys' suite with Tom and Alicia Landry, Tex and Marty Schramm, and Brandt.

Then on February 13, 1989, unaware of how near Jones was to buying the Cowboys, Johnson attended the Davey O'Brien Award banquet in Fort Worth. Landry and Schramm also were present. Twelve days later Johnson succeeded Landry.

These memories yielded a long-withheld chuckle from Schramm. He pondered one in particular.

"I've always wondered," he said, "what would have happened if I'd had Jimmy Johnson in place when Jones took over."

# Great Train Robbery

Jimmy Johnson was a faithful jogger. He covered two or three miles a day and walked back an equal or greater distance. The exercise cleared his mind, allowed him to think clearly and make bold decisions.

For example, two months on the job as Cowboys coach, he returned to their apartment and told Linda Kay, his wife of 26 years, "I want a divorce."

Months later, three winless games deep into a season en route to a 1–15 farcical closure, Johnson made another decision while jogging. This one sent tsunami waves through the NFL and liberated the Cowboys from a future of irrelevance.

This time, he divorced Herschel Walker.

Before Johnson reached that juncture, he confronted issues that led him to Walker's mega-trade. His legacy in terms of NFL-caliber talent was thin, as he analyzed and the record confirmed. But here and there lay ability unrefined only by immaturity and inexperience: Michael Irvin, Mark Tuinei, Nate Newton, Kevin Gogan, Bill Bates, Jim Jeffcoat, Eugene Lockhart, and Ken Norton Jr.

Johnson's first draft proved astonishingly smart. Troy Aikman off the top was an obvious choice. Thereafter came Daryl Johnston, Mark Stepnoski, and Tony Tolbert—all Pro Bowl caliber and eventual Super Bowl starters. Johnson's next deal started the layer of ice that existed between him and Aikman for two years.

He spent another No. 1 pick on All-American Steve Walsh, his Miami quarterback, in a supplemental draft. And in a blatant display of favoritism, Johnson drove to Dallas–Fort Worth (D-FW) Airport to greet Walsh and helped carry Walsh's luggage.

"He's something special," Johnson enthused. "He's a bottom-line quarterback. He knows how to win."

Indeed, with Aikman injured, Walsh was the only quarterback winner in '89 when the Cowboys beat Washington 13–3.

Johnson and owner Jerry Jones meantime were the roast of the town. Jones went trap-tongue again, saying the cheerleaders were "the pick of the litter," and Aikman, "looked good in the shower." A boomerang effect followed his claim that Johnson was worth five No. 1 draft picks and Heisman Trophy winners.

Critics shouted: Then trade him!

Johnson felt media fire at his feet. The Cowboys were swamped in his NFL debut in New Orleans, 28–0. Two losses later, Johnson pondered

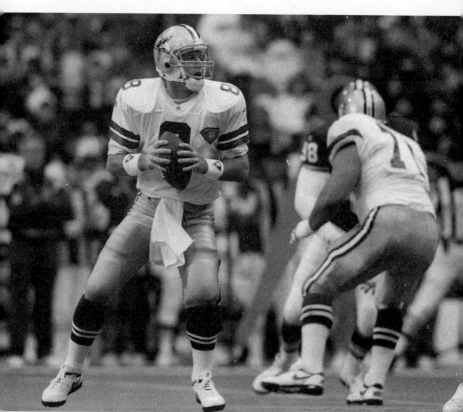

*Troy Aikman, here in 1994 action against Cleveland, was drafted in 1989 and became the winningest quarterback of any decade in NFL history.*

**DID YOU KNOW ...** That Jimmy Johnson was cocaptain of the undefeated Arkansas Razorbacks of 1964?

how to make the team better, quicker, because he saw it wasn't getting better any time soon.

He had one chip to play—star tailback Walker. Johnson parlayed him into a Spanish Armada of draft choices from the Minnesota Vikings: three No. 1s, three No. 2s, and a No. 3 through the 1990–1992 drafts.

That's how the trade panned out, but not how it looked to local scribes because of clauses too complicated to expand here. It appeared to them that the Cowboys got five worn-out players plus a No. 1 from Minnesota, failing to note that all five could and would be returned later for high draft choices.

"The Vikings got Herschel Walker. The Cowboys got nothing more than a huge handful of Minnesota smoke. And who knows if there'll ever be any fire," one columnist wrote.

"Love that steal for Minnesota. See you in the end zone, Herschel. See you later, Dallas. Much later."

The Cowboys weren't better, but they were not much worse without Walker. They were shut out three times, scored a team-record low 204 points, donated 27 interceptions, lost 15 fumbles, and had as their leading rusher one Paul Palmer with 446 yards.

One contentious incident interrupted the Cowboys' long slide into the nether region. Although never proven, Philadelphia's pugnacious coach, Buddy Ryan, was accused of putting bounties on the heads of kicker Luis Zendejas ($200) and Aikman ($500).

Johnson, who went 0–4 against Ryan, was incensed with Ryan after losing to the Eagles, 27–0, in a game labeled The Bounty Bowl.

"I would have said something to him but he wouldn't stay on the field long enough," Johnson fumed. "He got his fat rear end in the dressing room."

Bruised and battered by all comers, Aikman went 0–11 in his starts, but there were flashes where he rose above the surrounding muck. He set an NFL single game rookie record by passing for 379 yards in a 24–20 loss in Arizona. A microcosm of Aikman's season occurred when he threw a 75-yard touchdown to put Dallas ahead 21–17 with 1:43 left and was promptly knocked unconscious by a tackler.

The dreary march ended at home with a 20–10 defeat by Green Bay on an icy afternoon. It was cold enough to freeze toilet pipes in Texas Stadium, inspiring a wry epitaph from a local writer, "The season was so lousy it wouldn't even flush."

The press had been so negative one columnist went to Johnson days later to clarify that his criticism meant nothing personal. What he wrote was his professional opinion.

"Ah, hell, we were probably worse than you wrote," Johnson agreed.

Johnson would make 40-odd more trades, seine the Plan B free-agent market to find superb tight end Jay Novacek, and draft wisely. A gambling mentality—he's an ace at the blackjack table—suited Johnson, who was willing to bet big without fear of losing. When he did pull clunker trades for Danny Stubbs, Terrence Flagler, and Alonzo Highsmith, Johnson reacted smartly. He folded his hand quickly.

"I'm like the guy on the trapeze," he said. "He's got to fall to the net occasionally or nobody will come out to watch him."

Jones moved the Cowboys closer to observe when he left their training camp in temperate California in favor of blast-furnace Austin in '91. He also made it easier to turn a profit, as Johnson noted when he spied reams of sponsors' banners draped over fences around the field at St. Edward's University.

"This looks like a minor league baseball park," he grumbled. But after a pause, Johnson grinned and said, "But Jerry didn't get rich being dumb."

Johnson's smarts were displayed in the '90 draft when he used remnants of the Walker deal to move up four spots to 17th and claim Emmitt Smith. Thus 16 chances to pick the future all-time NFL rushing leader from Florida were spent on players of lesser value. Nor did anyone make the connection that The Triplets, as Aikman, Irvin, and Smith would be known, were now intact.

"He's as talented a back as I've ever been around," said Johnson after Smith rushed for 937 yards despite missing training camp and preseason during a contract holdout. "He's the type of back that puts you on the edge of your seat every time he touches the football."

# TRIVIA

Who was the other captain of the 1964 Arkansas Razorbacks?

*Answers to the trivia questions are on pages 163–164.*

Johnson made one trade he regretted even though he got more in return from New Orleans (Nos. 1 and 3 in '91, No. 2 in '92) than Walsh cost (a No. 1). But it left him uneasy if Aikman went down, which he did early in Game 15 with a shoulder injury. The position fell to rust-laden Babe Laufenberg, who'd played one quarter and one series over the previous two seasons.

The Cowboys were at 7-7, needing one victory to qualify as a wild card playoff entry and complete a stunning leap from 1-15. Laufenberg had no chance against Philadelphia (17-3) or Atlanta (26-7) when he threw a total of six interceptions.

Johnson came close to his seemingly laughable preseason goal ("I expect us to win as many as we lose") with a 7-9 finish. The near miss burned his impatient spirit anyway.

"I paid dearly for not having an adequate backup quarterback," he admitted. "If I'd had one, we probably would have gone from 1-15 in 1989 to the playoffs in 1990, and our turnaround would've come even faster and more obviously than it did."

Johnson still won an unprecedented honor as NFL Coach of the Year from the Associated Press. Never before had the AP award been given to a coach with a losing record. But Johnson was through coaching losing records.

His usual five-day vacation burned, Johnson prepared for the '91 season by acquiring Steve Beuerlein to caddy for Aikman. He nailed Russell Maryland, Alvin Harper, Erik Williams, Leon Lett, and Larry Brown in the draft, and delivered another prediction.

"Not only will we make the playoffs," he said, "but we will have success in the playoffs."

Johnson not only had tunnel vision about winning. He saw the future before it arrived.

# How 'Bout Those Cowboys!

Tex Schramm was elected to the Pro Football Hall of Fame in 1991, the only nonplayer-coach-owner-commissioner so honored. Tom Landry had been inducted a year earlier. While the NFL applauded the Old Era of the Cowboys, a revival was underway in the New Era.

The '91 Cowboys finished a wild card 11–5 and won a playoff game for the first time in nine years. This was the third consecutive year the team flew higher. Escaping the smog in '89 and breathing the postseason air left the Cowboys more comfortable.

"I believe we're just getting started," said coach Jimmy Johnson. "This is a very young team, and we are still developing."

A second-choice coaching hire helped speed the pace of progress. Johnson named Norv Turner of the Los Angeles Rams as offensive coordinator-quarterback coach. Johnson by then no longer spoke to Miami Dolphins aide Gary Stevens, who backed out after accepting his initial offer.

"Norv Turner was the winning link," Troy Aikman said years later. "I don't think we'd have won one Super Bowl, much less three, without Norv Turner."

Master motivator Johnson, a psychology major in college and as NFL coach, continued mind-game sermons. He believed in the power of persuasive thought. If he couldn't coach a team to victory he could talk it into winning.

"I wanted to establish the belief that we were going to win almost to the point of overachieving what we realistically could accomplish," he said. "It's a matter of attitude and, in some ways, almost brainwashing players—telling them time after time we'd be in the playoffs until, after a time, they began to believe it."

There were doubts among Johnson's congregation when the team wobbled at 6–5 and met 11–0 Washington, the eventual Super Bowl champion, at RFK Stadium. More so when, with Dallas ahead in the third quarter, 14–7, Aikman's season ended with a torn knee ligament.

But Johnson had patched that position with Steve Beuerlein, who coolly completed a 24–21 upset of the Redskins.

After which Beuerlein led four regular season victories and a 17–13 first round playoff win over Chicago before running afoul of Detroit, 38–6.

Previews of coming attractions were evident at season's end. Emmitt Smith (1,563 yards) and Michael Irvin (1,523 yards on 93 catches) became the first players on the same team to lead the NFL in rushing and receiving. Jay Novacek added a Pro Bowl–worthy and league-high 59 catches for tight ends.

Irvin's self-analysis spoke to the passion he brought to the game and why he earned the Playmaker nickname: "I've got to get better. I feel that if I'm standing still, somebody is catching up with me."

Johnson now could truthfully answer a question that dogged him during the 1–15 season. He had blown smoke in every press conference trying to protect what was left of team morale. Knowing otherwise, he kept insisting, "We are making progress."

On every occasion, the same columnist raised his hand and archly inquired, "Where?"

But now progress was apparent and measurable—a gain of 10 wins in the span of three seasons. Johnson wanted more, and thought it well within reach.

"In the preseason camp of '92 I knew we were good enough to win it all, if we could make steady progress through regular season and avoid the highs and lows that some teams go through, and then get on a roll in the playoffs," he reminisced.

The first opposing coach agreed that Johnson might be right. The Cowboys opened at home on *Monday Night Football* against defending Super Bowl champion Washington and fashioned a no-frills 23–10 victory.

## TRIVIA

**Who threw and who caught the longest nonscoring pass in club history, and how many yards did the play cover?**

*Answers to the trivia questions are on pages 163–164.*

*Jimmie Jones recovers a fumble near the Bills goal line and dives into the end zone in the Cowboys 52–17 rout of Buffalo in Super Bowl XXVII.*

"They are big, and they are strong, and they have good receivers," said Redskins coach Joe Gibbs. "They have an excellent defense. Excellent special teams. I think you have to say they are a heckuva team. They really are."

The defense had grown teeth with a trade for defensive end Charles Haley, the ferocious pass rusher from San Francisco with a reputation as an in-house scorpion. Johnson welcomed Haley as a difference-maker, which he proved to be, and used whip and chair to keep him under control.

As early as October 9, two days before the Cowboys walloped Seattle 27-0, Johnson spent four postdinner hours in Dallas absorbing how to prepare for a Super Bowl from a former NFL coach who'd won one. This coach had retired, pledged never to return, and was working as a TV analyst. Johnson's companion was Bill Parcells.

"By getting ready I mean all the logistics during the two-week stretch following the NFC championship game. I needed to know," Johnson recalled.

Other than a Game 4 stumble against Philadelphia, 31-7, a loss they twice reversed later, the Cowboys spewed club records en route to a 13-3 record and the first division title since 1985. The records were for most victories in a single season, Smith's NFL-leading 1,713 yards rushing, six offensive players named to the Pro Bowl, and largest pep rally (an estimated 68,000 at Texas Stadium) before the NFC championship game in San Francisco.

"We have more people here than most teams do at games," Irvin told the crowd. "That's why most teams are home and we're going to San Francisco. For those of you I don't see in San Francisco, I'll see you in Pasadena."

Candlestick Park was the scene of The Catch in '81 that beat the Cowboys 28-27, and the 49ers caught the scent of another potential rally with 4:22 left to play. They trailed 24-20 but had Dallas backed to its 21-yard line. Turner then made an aggressive play call that locked the game.

On first down he dialed a short Troy Aikman–to–Alvin Harper slant pass that Harper turned into a 70-yard gain. Aikman's six-yard touchdown dart to Kelvin Martin iced a 30-20 victory and a trip to the Super Bowl against Buffalo.

Johnson celebrated in the postgame locker room, shouting to his jubilant players, "How 'bout them Cowboys!"

A Rose Bowl crowd of 98,374 and a record 133.4 million TV viewers saw a halftime show starring Michael Jackson and a game dominated by the Cowboys. Aikman (22 of 30, 273 yards, four TDs) won the MVP award. The defense forced a glut of nine turnovers—four interceptions and five fumbles, two of them returned for short touchdowns by tackle Jimmie Jones and linebacker Ken Norton Jr.

Yet the 52–17 rout is recalled as often because the final score wasn't 59–17. If Leon Lett hadn't styled too soon on a 64-yard fumble rumble he would've added the padding. But before Lett reached the end zone, Don Beebe, in a display of supreme hustle in a long-lost cause, caught him and stripped the ball.

"We didn't shut them down in the first half, but we slowed them down," said stunned Bills linebacker Shane Conlan, recalling a 28–10 deficit at intermission. "I don't know what happened after that. It all went blank."

Johnson accomplished a rare triple. He became the only coach to win a national college title (Miami, 1987) and Super Bowl and to have played in a national champion (Arkansas, 1964).

"One of the reasons this is one of the happiest days of my life is that Jimmy and I went through that 1–15 season," said owner Jones. "We had some pretty low times together during that year, but I knew one day we'd be Super Bowl champions."

Tributes arrived from every direction. President Clinton phoned Johnson and fellow Arkansas native Jones to offer congratulations.

"He told me he thought the people of Arkansas were prouder of me than they were of him when he became president. I thanked him for the compliment but told him he was just being kind," Jones relayed.

How did the New Era do it? A retired NFL exec docked his fishing boat in Key West, Florida, and cited three elements he deemed most important.

"I think it's a great job. It's amazing, I would have to say," said former president/general manager Schramm.

**DID YOU KNOW . . .** That the longest touchdown pass in club playoff history was a 94-yard pass from Troy Aikman to Alvin Harper in the 1995 against Green Bay?

"One, they had a quarterback to start with in Aikman.

"Second, Johnson and his staff were great evaluators of personnel. They ran a lot of people through and knew what type of player they wanted and the player who fit that mold.

## TRIVIA

Who said, "The only person who can cover me one-on-one is my jersey"?

*Answers to the trivia questions are on pages 163–164.*

"The other is the great trade they made with Minnesota for Walker. That's one of the all-time great trades."

What now for the Cowboys, automatic favorites to win Super Bowl XXVIII?

"We're on top of the world," said elder Jim Jeffcoat, "and we're not coming off. You better be ready because we're going to be here for a long time."

Jeffcoat was right about the team as long-standing cream. All seemed right and bright with the Cowboys. Yet soon the house would be divided by internal strife that astounded and confounded the pro football world.

# The Rupture

*In the end, performed as a charade of mutual affection, Jerry Jones and Jimmy Johnson got what they wanted. They got rid of each other.*

*So they both won in a personal sense. Johnson has his freedom from an owner he cannot abide. Jones is free of Johnson, a coach he cannot trust.*

*Their parting after five years became official during a fanciful news conference at Valley Ranch. Johnson said he really did like Jones. Jones said he was extremely fond of Johnson. And the cow jumped over the moon.*

The Cowboys' pendulum forever swings. It just never stops on center. On March 29, 1994, it spun like a propeller as described in an excerpt from *The Dallas Morning News:*

> The franchise always has been a collection of extreme personalities, extravagant defeats and victories, in style and substance apart from all others. Its birthright is to be different, its fate to be unique, and its tradition to operate with flair.

But this was preposterous, beyond anything in the rich, varied history of the Cowboys or 75 years of NFL existence. In an emotional context, rapture introduced bizarre rupture. Owner and coach had scarcely finished celebrating their two-in-a-row Super Bowl champions that beat Buffalo, 30–13, in January.

In fact, the first postgame interview words from Jones praised Johnson. Johnson replied by thanking Jones for allowing him to do things his way. They even embraced.

"Jimmy told me later, under the steps, 'That tight hug I gave you...I meant it,'" Jones related.

In retrospect, this scene served as a rehearsal for the next charade when they split less than three months later. Johnson left for a beach condo in Florida with a $2 million severance check for the five years remaining on his contract. His willingness to abandon a team capable of winning one or two more Super Bowls, and Jones' unwillingness to talk him out of it, reflected the chasm of distance between them.

In one of sport's weirdest divorces, Jimmy got the beach condo and Jerry got to keep the kids, so to say.

The strain on their relationship had a deep taproot. Once above ground, it bloomed as poison ivy. Public perception—and near reality— was of Jones and Johnson constantly dueling for attention, praise, and credit. An underlay of friction bred by envy and pride of authorship increased until it flared into near open warfare.

Jibes and alleged jokes sprouted barbs before, during, and after victory in Super Bowl XXVIII in Atlanta. Late in the heat of a playoff run, Johnson said he was "interested" in an expansion franchise being settled in Jacksonville. He told the Super Bowl press he could be persuaded to coach elsewhere if the price and title were right, a newsy buzz that went national.

Someone asked about the Apex television commercial in which Jones was hitchhiking and is left covered in road dust by Johnson's speeding auto. Johnson said he didn't know the plot in advance.

"Jerry's the one who had the idea to not pick him up. I guess he wanted to make the commercial as realistic as possible," Johnson laughed.

Jones had his moments, too. He said he could coach the Cowboys as well as Johnson, although he'd rather not. He ranked his duties of negotiating contracts and marketing the team "as important as a defensive coordinator." Then there was his stinger that the Cowboys were so powerful that "500 coaches could have won the Super Bowl."

Neither would have advanced to Atlanta if Emmitt Smith hadn't twice rescued the 1993 season that Leon Lett almost sabotaged. His first relief act

## TRIVIA

En route to a 30–13 Super Bowl XXVIII victory over Buffalo, what team held the Cowboys to 10 points—the fewest number they scored during the regular season?

*Answers to the trivia questions are on pages 163–164.*

135

*The MVP of Super Bowl XXVIII was the Cowboys Emmitt Smith, here sweeping to his right against the Bills in the Cowboys' 30–13 win.*

was to end a contract holdout. The Cowboys were 0–2 when he reappeared, one loss a 13–10 dump by Buffalo.

No team had ever escaped from that deep a ditch to reach the Super Bowl. Smith's presence jump-started a seven-game winning streak before another crisis left the Cowboys in shaky shape at 7–4. A loss to Atlanta preceded Lett's loopy play that donated a 16–14 victory to Miami.

Conditions were surreal, the natural setting for Lett, who'd made a rundown hero of Don Beebe in the previous Super Bowl. A freak November sleet and snowstorm applied ice-rink slickness to Texas Stadium's floor. Thus a slippery carpet assisted Lett's skid into further ignominy.

Teammates waved to let a blocked field goal die around their goal line to end the game with Dallas ahead, 14–13. But shy, introverted Lett kept galloping. He slid into the ball and nudged a recovery by the Dolphins who kicked a last-play, decisive 19-yard field goal.

A four-game winning spurt then sent the Cowboys to New York against the Giants to determine the NFC East title. Elite players rise to the occasion in games of this magnitude. Great ones rise above it.

So it was that Smith's supreme hour played out at Giants Stadium in the form of a 16–13 overtime victory.

Smith's right shoulder had been dislocated in the second quarter. Yet he played on, and the longer the better. Running and catching on nine plays, he gained 41 of 52 overtime yards needed for Eddie Murray's clinching, 20-yard field goal.

Emmitt rushed 32 times for 168 yards on a painfully cold day made worse by an aching shoulder. He caught 10 passes for 61 yards, setting a club record for most rushing and receiving attempts (42) in a single game. Every highlight review of Smith's career begins with this heroic performance.

The 12–4 division champs beat Green Bay 27–17 and San Francisco 38–21 in playoffs. Victory over the 49ers was even guaranteed to a sports radio host accustomed to hometown fans shouting, "We will win the game!" But this call-in voice didn't belong to a fan. It was the hometown coach, Johnson.

"Well, the man's got balls, I'll say that," responded 49ers coach George Seifert. "I don't know if they're brass or papier-mâché. We'll find out pretty soon."

Two Cowboys dominated Super Bowl XXVIII and finished one-two in the MVP vote. Smith won it, gaining 91 of his 132 yards in the second half, which began with Buffalo ahead 13–6. Other honors such as MVP of the NFL and All-Pro would follow.

Free safety James Washington was as worthy an MVP candidate. He forced one fumble that led to a field goal, scored on a 46-yard fumble return to create a tie at 13-all, and picked a Jim Kelly pass to set up another touchdown. Involvement in three turnovers plus a team-high 10 solo tackles still placed him a debatable MVP runner-up to Smith.

The armistice between Jones and Johnson, signified by their post–Super Bowl embrace, proved of short duration.

## TRIVIA

**What was Jimmy Johnson's record as head coach of the Cowboys?**

*Answers to the trivia questions are on pages 163–164.*

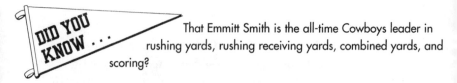

That Emmitt Smith is the all-time Cowboys leader in rushing yards, rushing receiving yards, combined yards, and scoring?

The incident that sealed their divorce occurred on the evening of March 23 during a party at the owner's meeting in Orlando.

Jones was basking in his dual role of king of the Cowboys and owner of two Super Bowl trophies. A festive air prevailed as guests made generous use of the bar. A handshaking tour took Jones to a table where Johnson was telling an unflattering story about him to a group of current and former Cowboy employees.

An unwelcome Jones raised his glass and proposed a toast, "Here's to the Dallas Cowboys, and here's to the people who made it possible to win two Super Bowls!"

No one at the table responded. Two were people Jones had fired. Jones repeated his toast and again received no reaction.

"You [blank] people just go on with your [blank] party," Jones snapped, and walked off.

Later that night, or rather early the next morning in a hotel watering hole, Jones told two *Dallas Morning News* reporters that he planned to fire Johnson. Six days later he did it.

Johnson much later put a mellow spin on his exit as it related to Jones, who caught maximum scorn in the aftermath. Seven years had elapsed. He'd become a TV analyst for NFL games after coaching the Miami Dolphins for four seasons.

"I really have tremendous respect for Jerry. I consider him a friend," said Johnson without sounding facetious. "As much as anything I was ready to leave. I wanted to live in south Florida.

"Jerry can't be blamed for that. I thought he was out of line for some of the things he said and did. But he can't be blamed for me leaving. If not that year it would have been the next year. There was never a point where I was going to stay forever.

"Jerry did throw gas on the fire. Maybe he did it because he sensed I'd given him the idea I wasn't staying."

But who would follow Johnson? Jones knew. He made a late night call from Orlando to alert the successor.

# Coach Gunsmoke

The telephone call from Jerry Jones found Barry Switzer taking a shower at his home in Norman, Oklahoma. When Jones asked if he had interest in coaching the Cowboys, a dripping wet Switzer was so startled that he dropped his towel.

He became the only coach of the Cowboys hired in the nude.

Switzer's first reaction, after picking up the towel, was bafflement that Jones and Jimmy Johnson had split.

"But what the hell is going on?" Switzer asked Jones. "Why can't you guys get along? I just want to know how ya'll two screwed up one of the greatest things in the NFL. Hell, Jerry, you just won your second Super Bowl."

Switzer next expressed gratitude at the offer.

"Frankly, I thought my time had passed," he admitted. "But when Jerry asked if I was interested, I said, 'Who in America wouldn't be? Who wouldn't want to coach the best team with the best coaching staff and the best players?'"

Apparently no one except Jones wanted that coach to be Switzer. The list included players who were disciples of Johnson.

"This makes me rethink about my intentions of coming back to the Cowboys," guard Kevin Gogan promised, and left to join the Oakland Raiders.

"I'll take 50 percent of him [Johnson] rather than 100 percent of most coaches," Michael Irvin grumbled.

Critics leaped from behind faraway logs to pile on. Retired 49ers coach Bill Walsh referred to Switzer as a "ceremonial" coach, mocking his perceived house-pet servitude to Jones.

*Jerry Jones, aching to prove that he could win a Super Bowl without Jimmy Johnson, handed the head coaching duties to former Oklahoma legendary head coach Barry Switzer, here holding the Lombardi Trophy the Cowboys earned by beating Pittsburgh 27–17 in Super Bowl XXX.*

As for Jones, the Switzer deal squandered the last gram of public approval gained by inducting Tom Landry into the Ring of Honor last November. Lobbied by former players to accept requests he'd previously ignored, Landry stiffly endured the ceremony alongside the owner who fired him.

As for Switzer, he once stood atop his profession at the college level. He won three national championships at Oklahoma and had a brilliant 157–29–4 record. However, a series of player scandals forced his ouster in 1989 and tainted his reputation so severely that he became a coaching pariah.

His NFL credentials were shaky since there weren't any. As an added tactical negative to five years of idleness, Switzer's last football experience was running a Wishbone offense.

Switzer also faced parochial bias as a figure from the wrong side of the inflamed Red River Rivalry between OU and the University of Texas. Old grudges existed from a bygone year when Longhorns coach Darrell Royal accused Switzer's staff of spying on practices. Smug satisfaction lingered when the charge later was proven true.

Switzer was thus doomed from the outset as unacceptable and irrelevant. Not that it bothered his cheery persona.

"I don't have enough time left to have a bad time," said the 56-year-old.

Switzer knew many bad times. He was born dirt-floor poor in Arkansas. The family home had no electricity, running water, or telephone when he left for college. An accident and a suicide took both parents from Switzer's life.

His bootlegger father burned to death in a fiery car wreck. The vehicle, en route to the hospital, was driven by a remorseful girlfriend who had shot him. High on prescription drugs and alcohol, his mother shot herself on the back porch after Barry and his brother resisted her fumed attempts to kiss them good night, leaving Switzer guilt-stricken for decades.

This baggage was long buried when Switzer made a peppy appearance as the third coach in Cowboys history.

## TRIVIA

**When Emmitt Smith rushed for a team record 1,773 yards in 1995, whose record did he break?**

*Answers to the trivia questions are on pages 163–164.*

That Barry Switzer won 84 percent of his games as head coach at Oklahoma, fourth best all-time?

"Nothing is going to change. Get ready to watch the Dallas Cowboys be the best team in the NFL. We got a job to do and we're going to do it, baby!" he exclaimed.

Switzer was an easy man to play for and coach under. He was repelled by abusive methods coaches used to motivate players. His coaxing style at first drew approval in contrast to the harping pressure applied by Johnson. In terms of results, it worked for two years.

In '94 the Cowboys sailed again to the NFC Championship in Candlestick Park, only to run aground. Five turnovers led to an early 21–0 deficit and 38–28 loss. A last chance rally in the final six minutes expired when Switzer drew a penalty for unsportsmanlike conduct. He bumped an official to illustrate how Deion Sanders of the 49ers got away with mugging Michael Irvin at the San Francisco 10-yard line.

"I threw my hip into him and said, 'You mean this is not interfering?' and he threw his flag," Switzer replayed. "Sure, it was a mistake that I gave them 15 yards. I contributed to us getting beat, no question."

Well, maybe. The Cowboys were still behind by the final 10 points. Switzer's candor, becoming rare for a coach, went unappreciated. Jones meantime spoke to the ghost who overhung defeat. "I think there definitely will be speculation as to what we could have done out there if Jimmy were the coach," he admitted.

Aikman's admission touched the truth. "We came in here as champs and we are, until proven otherwise. Today it was proven otherwise," he said.

Switzer capped his rookie NFL season with an incident that upset purists. Coaching the NFC in the Pro Bowl in Hawaii, he ate a hot dog on the sideline during the game. His image as a hood ornament enlarged further.

The year was memorable for the franchise, anyway. Tony Dorsett and Randy White were inducted into the Pro Football Hall of Fame and the Ring of Honor. The Cowboys tied their record total of 11 players in the Pro Bowl, among them bemused fullback Daryl Johnston, career-long blocker for Emmitt Smith.

"I've probably got the worst stats of anybody who's ever gone to the Pro Bowl," said Johnston, referring to his best rushing day of 60 yards. "I don't think there's ever been a back who has gained fewer than 100 yards [in a game] and still made the Pro Bowl."

Jones prepared for the '95 season with customary bravado. He created headlines by raiding the 49ers for cornerback/punt return ace/major league baseball outfielder Deion Sanders. The $35 million contract included a $12.999 million signing bonus, proof that Jones would spend to win.

The team was grimly determined, stout enough to finish 12–4 and win its fourth consecutive NFC East title. Smith left rushing-scoring records in his wake: a team-best 1,773 yards and an all-time NFL high of 25 touchdowns.

Oh, there was one messy episode in Philadelphia and naturally Switzer was involved. He twice called "Load Left," from the Dallas 29 in the dying minutes of a tie game, and Smith was stuffed on fourth down plunges both times.

The Eagles used that gift position to kick a field goal and win, 20–17. After which the *New York Post* referred to Switzer as Bozo the Coach. Switzer and Jones were labeled Dumb and Dumber.

Not so after the Cowboys drilled the Eagles in a first-round playoff, 30–11, dusted Green Bay, 38–27, and advanced to Super Bowl XXX against Pittsburgh in Tempe, Arizona. But Switzer knew this still wasn't good enough. Acid reviews would flow if he didn't win with what was perceived as Johnson's team.

"If I don't, I'm a failure. I accept that," he said, failing to mention 27 of his players were Super Bowl rookies.

But Switzer's cheery persona didn't allow him to dwell on the negative. He even prepared a postgame message for critics.

"After the game, if we win, I'm going to tell them the good news is we won the game. The bad news is I'm coming back," he chuckled.

**DID YOU KNOW . . .** That Barry Switzer was an assistant coach for his alma mater, Arkansas, and coached both Jerry Jones and Jimmy Johnson?

Others felt more pressure judging by a remark from Neil O'Donnell. The Pittsburgh quarterback cancelled Mondays from future calendars when he said, "After Sunday, there is no tomorrow."

Sunday remained an overcast day for O'Donnell, who threw three interceptions. MVP cornerback Larry Brown picked him twice, the game-clincher a sideline peg blamed on the quarterback but the actual fault of a receiver who ran the wrong route.

Thus via a 27–17 victory the Cowboys became the first team in NFL history to win three Super Bowls in a four-year span. Yet to Aikman, sensitive to creeping spoilage within the team, joy was tempered by overwhelming relief.

"I've never been so happy for a season to end in all my life," he said.

Did Switzer feel vindicated?

"No, I don't care. They'll just reload again when I stumble," he said.

Before he was turned out Switzer fell long and hard, arrested at D-FW Airport for wearing a concealed handgun he'd forgotten to unpack. As he neared the end of his term with the Cowboys he was no longer Bozo the Coach. He had become Coach Gunsmoke.

# Bye-Bye Barry

Easy ways don't work during hard times. Lack of firm discipline acceptable to a winner becomes unendurable for a loser plagued by thin drafts and free agent flops, injuries, and age.

The Cowboys image began to change, and none of it for the better. Youthful exuberance morphed into mature arrogance. The boorish behavior of a few sank franchise image to a historic low. America's Team became America's embarrassment.

The signs were there before and during Super Bowl XXX and climaxed afterward. As kings often do, a group of players were overcome by delusions of supremacy.

Rather than ride the team bus to practice, Michael Irvin, Erik Williams, Leon Lett, and Nate Newton hired a $1,000-per-day stretch limousine to deliver them in regal style. Lett had missed four games in '95 serving his second of three eventual suspensions for a substance-abuse violation. Irvin opened the '96 season suspended for five games for the same violation.

Scandal peaked with discovery of a party house where players-only mingled with women of dubious character. All of it happened on Barry Switzer's watch, and in '97 he even contributed with the concealed handgun incident at D-FW Airport, for which owner Jerry Jones levied a $75,000 fine.

Public opinion judged Switzer responsible by assumption as a repeat of the episodes that led to his ouster at Oklahoma University. Yet one last 10–6 charge in '96 promoted him to a unique position no one would have predicted. Switzer reigns as the last Cowboys coach to win a playoff.

The date: December 28. The site: Texas Stadium. The wild card game result: Dallas 40, Minnesota 15.

# TRIVIA

**Who is the only Cowboy to score touchdowns on a run from scrimmage, pass reception, punt return, and kickoff return in his career?**

*Answers to the trivia questions are on pages 163–164.*

Visions of extending the season ended the next week on the second play of a divisional playoff at Carolina. Irvin caught a 22-yard pass and left the game with a dislocated right shoulder.

The abrupt loss of their leading receiver pulled half the teeth from an offense that mustered one touchdown during a 26–17 defeat.

A team that appeared frayed came apart in '97. Morale bottomed. Beginning in '93, consecutive top draft choices Shante Carver, Sherman Williams, Kavika Pittman, and David LaFleur proved non-impact additions. Guard Larry Allen and linebacker Dexter Coakley were the only worthwhile pickups in later rounds.

The swoon was widespread. Emmitt Smith rushed for 1,074 yards, the lowest total since his rookie season in '90. Aikman was sacked 33 times, the most in seven years. The defense tied a team low record for fewest interceptions (seven) in a single season.

Relapse evolved into surrender down the stretch. A 6–10 season ended forlornly on a five-game losing note.

"This didn't happen overnight," Aikman said. "We've been declining the last couple of years to where we are now. But I think we're better than 6–10. We didn't play as well as our talent would indicate we would."

Switzer had to go. That was a given. Even he agreed.

"I told Jerry he ought to get rid of the whole damn bunch of us," he announced.

Switzer's departure was greeted as the exit of a caricature rather than a coach. Jones reduced him to that perception with sideline scenes of whispering into Switzer's ear as if imparting strategy. Jones also assumed the authority of a coach in updating injuries and starting positions. He criticized defensive coaches at midseason, sat in on their film study, once entered the coaches' press box during a game, and admitted dreams of coaching himself.

Jones created further shudders with a late-season edict on how the team would function in the future.

"The best chance for us to continue with the success we've enjoyed is to do it our way—by that I mean *my* way," he said.

The owner lost his way the first time he tried to hire Switzer's successor. His search was four weeks long when it isolated former UCLA coach Terry Donohue as the target. But amid reports of a done deal, Donohue rejected the job.

Jones settled on Chan Gailey, Pittsburgh Steelers offensive coordinator and two-year head coach of Birmingham in the World League of American Football. Quiet-spoken, 46-year-old Gailey was regaled as a savant on offense. In an ironic twist, his ideas of revamping the offense were the source of his being rejected by members of that unit.

An early visitor to Gailey's office asked if he'd sought advice from peers before accepting the position.

*Michael Irvin, here celebrating a touchdown reception against Green Bay in the 1996 NFC championship game, holds most Cowboys all-time receiving records.*

DID YOU KNOW . . . That Troy Aikman is the all-time Cowboys' leader in passing attempts, completions, yards, and touchdowns?

"I was told I had to take the job," he said, meaning the promotion was a professional imperative. And?

"That Jerry was very involved."

Gailey didn't infer that he accepted the role of serf to His Royal Jones. He just understood that Jones was interested in his socks-to-jocks way.

"I don't understand this talk about me being intimidated," he said. "Am I supposed to act differently when he's in here? He didn't hire me to be somebody who drops to a knee every time he enters a room. I have to do what's best for this team because if I don't, I'll be looking myself in the mirror 10 years from now and telling myself that I didn't give myself a chance."

Two-thirds of the Triplets were ecstatic at Gailey's presence.

"I will surprise people. Chan will surprise people. And when we get it going again, they're going to fear us, just like they used to, because we have guys capable of making plays. I think this club is going to turn the 6–10 completely around," said Smith.

Aikman gave Gailey a qualified endorsement in terms of returning structure and discipline. He withheld judgment on how Gailey promised to alter the offense, which included adding Deion Sanders to the lineup as a receiver, an idea that neither former offensive coordinator Ernie Zampese nor Aikman embraced.

Aikman's wait-and-see attitude was justified. He eventually lost faith in Gailey's overall approach.

"From what I have seen so far," Aikman granted, "I think we are giving ourselves as good a chance as we could, which I don't think we did the last couple of years. If nothing else, there appears to be a sense of accountability and I think that is what everyone wants—for everyone to be accountable."

Aikman was in tune with Gailey if he no longer tolerated a culture of shortcuts and sloth. A perfectionist, the quarterback admitted he allowed those in-house factors to distract his performance.

"I let a lot of things affect my play negatively that were beyond my control," he said. "It influenced my attitude to the point where I wasn't able to go out and do my best and let the rest take care of itself. It was a very frustrating few years for me and I wasn't enjoying the game as much as I should."

Irvin had no qualms about the new coach.

"Yeah, we're finished, we're too old, our time is gone," he mocked. "Chan is doing everything right. He's what we needed. People who want to bury us better hold off with the shovels."

Jones was still in shock over the collapse of '97. He trusted Aikman, more than anyone, as the key talent in restoring the team's championship form. While this belief had merit, it soon influenced Jones to make a decision that set back franchise growth for at least three years.

"When we had a healthy Troy Aikman last season and you wake up and the cold shock of having won only six games hits you in the face, it becomes unthinkable," Jones said. "We can't let that happen again."

Nor did it happen during Gailey's maiden season.

# The Football Man

All the endorsements of Chan Gailey appeared justified when his debut season produced a 10–6 record and an NFC title, the Cowboys sixth in the last seven years. Emmitt Smith proved a prophet when he forecast a reverse of the 6–10 finish from the previous season.

Smith was a man under the microscope as he continued pursuit of Tony Dorsett's team career rushing record. On November 8, in Texas Stadium against the New York Giants, he overtook Dorsett's 12,036-yard total and kept going. With 12,566 yards at season's end, Emmitt Smith stood fifth on the NFL's all-time rushing chart.

Nor was he finished setting records.

The next one was for the most career rushing touchdowns in NFL history, a mark held by Marcus Allen at 123. Smith passed Allen with a one-yard dive against Washington on December 20, added a 26-yard scoring canter, and closed the season with 125.

One-man-act Deion Sanders produced another show that naturally starred Prime Time. In a September game against the Giants he returned a punt 59 yards for a touchdown and ran back an interception 71 yards to score again. It was the first time in club history that one player scored two touchdowns on returns in the same game.

These sparkles, mingled with a division title, sustained Gailey's reputation among his peers.

"The Cowboys couldn't have picked a better guy. Chan is the perfect man for the job," touted Denver coach Mike Shanahan, the Broncos quarterback coach when Gailey served alongside as offensive coordinator.

"I think Dallas is getting a very good coach and someone who is going to be an excellent head coach," Pittsburgh's Bill Cowher agreed.

Denver quarterback John Elway's praise was well intentioned but over time proved inaccurate when he said, "Troy is going to enjoy working with him as I did during his days here in Denver. I think you're going to see that he's going to be one of the great coaches in this league."

**TRIVIA**

**Who made up the "Triplets"?**

*Answers to the trivia questions are on pages 163–164.*

As former coach Barry Switzer warned after each victory, humility lurks only seven days away. So it was with Gailey when his top-heavy favored Cowboys met 9–7 Arizona at home in a wild card playoff. The day ended in humiliation.

This was an opponent the Cowboys beat twice during the regular season by scores of 38–10 and 35–28. Nor had the Cardinals won a playoff since 1947 when they were located in Chicago. Yet against a franchise making its 25th postseason appearance, Arizona pulled a jarring 20–7 upset.

If there was a peak in Gailey's brief tenure, it followed in the 1999 season opener in Washington where the Cowboys trailed 35–14 after three periods. A 21-point fourth quarter sent the game into overtime and on a daring call by Gailey, Aikman threw a 76-yard touchdown pass to Raghib Ismail to win 41–35.

Just as quickly, the season fell apart when the Cowboys rolled into Philadelphia with a 3–0 record. Michael Irvin caught an eight-yard pass, the 750th of his career, and never played again. Neck and back injuries ushered him out of the game at age 33, ranking ninth all-time in receiving yards (11,904) and 10th all-time in receptions.

The season fluttered until it ended at 8–8 with a 27–10 wild card loss to Minnesota. The only sop was watching Smith gain 99 yards to surpass Franco Harris as the NFL's career postseason rushing leader with a 1,586-yard total.

Friction now existed between Gailey and veterans who resisted his altered offensive schemes. The freeze with Aikman was so acute Gailey avoided late-season quarterback meetings. The coach had to be replaced, and he was when owner Jerry Jones promoted defensive coordinator Dave Campo.

"I don't think Chan had an idea of what the job entailed, but I thought he was a good head coach," Aikman said after he retired. "He tried to put

# TRIVIA

**Who holds the Cowboys record for the longest return of a fumble?**

*Answers to the trivia questions are on pages 163–164.*

his stamp on the club. Of all the coaches I had over 12 years, he was the only one who brought back former players to help bridge the gap in generations. "We had philosophical differences because the offense we'd run for seven years won three Super Bowls. Chan's offense was completely different. I had a hard time adjusting to that."

Aikman had seen the franchise rise from bottom to top and begin a descent into mediocrity. He cited two reasons for the downward shift.

"We lost discipline as a club and we didn't do a good job of replacing talent we were losing," he said and moved to the issue of tangled lines of authority under Jones. "Everyone shares the responsibility to some degree. Who's ultimately responsible? I don't know if there are clear lines of responsibility at Valley Ranch [the Cowboys' training facility]. It's not easy to pinpoint who's responsible for what."

Jones decided it was he. He became The Football Man. A self-destructive optimist, his nature is to see blue skies within a mushroom cloud and Super Bowl trophies in the next box of Cracker Jacks.

This explained his belief that all his team needed for an all-the-way dash was to pair Aikman with a fast receiver. So Jones peddled two No. 1 draft choices to Seattle for Joey Galloway, who tore a knee ligament in Game 1 and never played another down in 2000.

That trade continued to haunt the Cowboys throughout the coming decade. Loss of those high choices practically voided their next two drafts. Ever since, Jones has faced the unwelcome reminder that Shaun Alexander, 2005 MVP of the NFL, was chosen by Seattle with a pick from the Galloway deal.

The Aikman-Galloway duo was but a passing fancy. Aikman retired after the 2000 season, his career-ender a concussion dished out by Washington linebacker LaVar Arrington at Texas Stadium on December 10. He and Galloway played together a total of 14 games plus a few minutes.

Jones, The Football Man, wasn't through. He ignored scouting advice on the second round in 2001 to draft quarterback Quincy Carter, a player no other NFL team ranked that high. The reasons became

*As driven a man who ever played pro football, Emmitt Smith's passion for the game and talent were rewarded when he set the all-time NFL rushing record in this game against Seattle on October 27, 2002.*

**By the NUMBERS**

**1**—All-time rank in rush attempts, rushing yards, and touchdowns by Emmitt Smith

**2**—All-time rank in yards from scrimmage and rushing/receiving touchdowns by Emmitt Smith

**4.2**—Career rushing average for Emmitt Smith

**7**—Emmitt Smith's place in Heisman Trophy voting in 1989

**15**—Emmitt Smith's years playing in the NFL

**19**—Emmitt Smith's career postseason touchdowns

**132**—Emmitt Smith's yards rushed in Super Bowl XXVIII

**164**—Emmitt Smith's career touchdowns

**1,586**—Emmitt Smith's career postseason rushing yards

**18,355**—Emmitt Smith's career rushing yards

evident over the next three seasons, all wasted in a futile attempt to develop Carter.

Poor, likeable Campo had no chance. He lasted three years of repetitive 5–11 records. With Jones calling the shots, quarterbacks replicated the march of the penguins. Jones signed veteran Tony Banks and then, unhappy with his practice habits, cut him in training camp. Carter was thrown in the briar patch as a rookie.

Thereafter came Anthony Wright, Randall Cunningham, Clint Stoerner, and Ryan Leaf. All came and went.

"I've been coaching here a year and a half and I'm getting my seventh quarterback ready," sighed quarterback coach Wade Wilson, whose pupils began with Aikman. "There's something different every week."

Jones did everything short of adopting Carter to prove he could spot talent. Jittery and unsure of himself, Carter reacted badly to internal competition. He blew himself out of the starting job during a 9–6 loss to Arizona in 2002. Carter threw four interceptions, two in the end zone, and pitched a temper fit on the sideline.

"When we win this game, ya'll are going to give me more reps," he screamed, inferring he didn't get enough repetitions in practice and didn't want to share any. Jones was on the sideline and got in Carter's face.

"He was saying, 'I can play better than this, if you get me the reps,'"
Jones said. "His tone of voice said, 'The interceptions wouldn't have happened if I got all the snaps.' I'm thinking, 'Let's not go there.'"

Carter later became an expensive footnote in Cowboy history, a
player who betrayed the owner who placed so much faith in him. The
dreary Campo years between 2000–2002 saw Aikman retire, Bob Hayes
inducted into the Ring of Honor, and former coach Tom Landry die of
leukemia at age 75.

The lone magnet during this drought was Smith as he closed the gap
on the NFL's all-time rushing leader, Walter Payton. Emmitt reached the
pinnacle in 2002 against Seattle in Texas Stadium with a burst of 11 yards
to move past Payton's mark of 16,726. Smith put the season to bed by
extending his record to 17,162 yards.

A composite 15–33 record over the last three seasons called for a
dramatic coaching change. Jones obliged with a hire that rattled the NFL.

# The Big Tuna

Jerry Jones hired Bill Parcells to coach the Cowboys on January 3, 2003, a decision interpreted to mean The Football Man at Valley Ranch admitted he needed help. Mutual need inspired Parcells to provide it.

But how could they coexist? The issue of compatibility overhung their potentially volatile partnership.

Parcells agreed to work for an owner with a long nose that previous coaches found stuck in their business. Jones opted to partner with a bullheaded coach known to resent any intrusion onto his turf. Locals activated The Friction Watch for signs of clash between these mega-egos.

What most analysts missed was the common agenda and purpose that linked them. Both were in their early sixties. The joke was they were closer to the Senior Bowl than the Super Bowl.

Their agenda was to prove that geezers could still do it. Their purpose was to succeed in a hurry. A schedule of opponents included the clock and calendar.

"We don't have time or inclination to get into minor bickering. Time is our No. 1 challenge," Jones said. "I'm not looking at where and what we'll be in 10 years. We've got a job to do now."

Parcells knew this would be his last rodeo. So why saddle up with Jones? Indeed, Jones was a pivotal factor in his decision to mount a final comeback. From behind his desk at Valley Ranch, the new coach nodded toward the owner's office to explain his presence.

"Because of him," he said. "He's committed to win. Not all of them [owners] are."

There was another reason he chose to leave a network TV gig and coach again.

"It's who I am. It's what I do," Parcells said.

Parcells did it well in the past, winning Super Bowls XXI and XXV with the New York Giants, and guiding New England to Super Bowl XXXI. He also brought a history of abrupt exits from those jobs and a tendency to announce false retirements.

Jones owned three Super Bowl trophies but like Parcells, memories of his glory days were aged enough to require carbon dating. He'd become the focal point for failure by fans and media. One wit accused Jones of clinging to "delusions of adequacy."

*Looking to resurrect the Cowboys, Jerry Jones hired proven winner Bill Parcells, here against New Orleans in 2004, to become only the sixth head coach in Dallas history.*

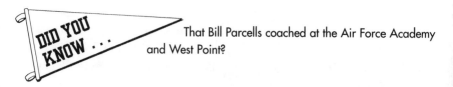

That Bill Parcells coached at the Air Force Academy and West Point?

No one quarreled with his choice of Parcells, who made first contact about the job through an intermediary. Someone noted that Parcells was the first head coach Jones hired who had previous NFL head coaching experience. Jones elaborated on that point in comparing the learning curves of two of his former coaches.

"Bill is an NFL pro football coach. What happened with Jimmy [Johnson] is he had to get there. Jimmy was so smart he got there quickly. While he was getting there, Bill was piling it on," Jones said. "As for Barry [Switzer], no question that Barry had to start from scratch in the NFL."

The issue of compatibility with an authority figure like Parcells lay dormant in the owner's mind. He believed age and experience had taught both to avoid conflict through compromise.

"I've been at this 14 years. Bill has been at it for 30-odd years. We know what to look out for. Contrary to what many people think, I had more emotional disagreements with Switzer than Jimmy," Jones said.

So went the prelude to a 2003 season that tested public emotions when the Cowboys bade farewell to two franchise icons. Emmitt Smith was released in February en route to career's end in Arizona two forget-table years later. Tex Schramm, 83, died in July, three months prior to his posthumous entry into the Ring of Honor.

Parcells and defensive coordinator Mike Zimmer then worked magic to produce a wild card qualifying 10–6 record that defied logic and the talent at hand. Zimmer fielded the NFL's No. 1–ranked defense, and it had to be that good. The offense, shut out twice, scored only one touch-down in six games. The total moved to seven games after a 29–10 playoff loss to Carolina.

Parcells got it done with Quincy Carter, his definition of a bus driver at quarterback, and a speedy defense held together by wise veteran Darren Woodson at strong safety. Sudden success intoxicated. Even Parcells felt chesty enough at midseason to ask his players, "Who out there scares you?"

Ah, who once said, "Success is never final, and failure is never fatal?" It was Barry Switzer, and his remark about the shelf life of success fit the

2004 Cowboys. The tires, wheels, and the rims of their season came off before it began.

Dawn brought drama to the Midwestern University training camp in Wichita Falls. Carter was released for reasons never publicly specified because of a privacy clause in the collective bargaining agreement. Multiple sources confirmed that substance abuse violations and lesser issues led to his dismissal.

The starting job fell to ancient Vinnie Testaverde, 42 in November, supposedly a backup. Except for flashes from rookie Julius Jones—a third-best-ever 198 yards rushing against Seattle and a tight end club record 87 catches by Jason Witten—the offense stumbled.

Woodson's ailing back failed to mend. The team's career leading tackler (1,350) never played, retired in December, and by then the defense had cratered without him. From a yield of 260 points the year before, the Cowboys leaked a club record 405.

Parcells walked through the season-ending locker room of a 6–10 disaster swearing, "There'll be changes around here!"

Jones granted his wish. Indeed, if Parcells had a Christmas wish list for 2005, Jones played Santa Claus. The owner didn't empty his wallet but he shook it vigorously.

Out tumbled free agent cornerback Anthony Henry, nose tackle Jason Ferguson, and guard Marco Rivera at a combined cost of $28 million in just signing bonuses. Drew Bledsoe, Parcells' quarterback when the Patriots reached the Super Bowl, also came aboard.

## TRIVIA

**At what Texas college did Bill Parcells once coach?**

Answers to the trivia questions are on pages 163–164.

"When it comes to these kinds of decisions, I will do what it takes to get us to the Super Bowl," Jones said.

And even host a Super Bowl in 2009. Voters in Arlington approved a stadium referendum in November to help fund a retractable roof stadium with the capacity for 90,000 customers. The site lies midway between Dallas and Fort Worth near Six Flags Over Texas and the Texas Rangers' baseball stadium.

The Arlington ballot followed October's one-man vote (Jones) that welcomed Rayfield Wright and Cliff Harris into the Ring of Honor. Both were members of the NFL's All-Decade Team of the '70s and, with Bob

All-Time
Cowboys

## Silver Season All-Time Team 1969–1985
### (as voted by fans)

### Offense

| | |
|---|---|
| QB | Don Meredith |
| | Roger Staubach |
| RB | Tony Dorsett |
| | Walt Garrison |
| | Don Perkins |
| C | John Fitzgerald |
| G | John Niland |
| | Herb Scott |
| T | Ralph Neely |
| | Rayfield Wright |
| TE | Billy Joe DuPree |
| WR | Bob Hayes |
| | Drew Pearson |
| K | Rafael Septien |
| P | Danny White |

### Defense

| | |
|---|---|
| DE | Ed Jones |
| | Harvey Martin |
| DT | Bob Lilly |
| | Randy White |
| LB | Chuck Howley |
| | Lee Roy Jordan |
| | D. D. Lewis |
| CB | Cornell Green |
| | Mel Renfro |
| | Everson Walls |
| S | Cliff Harris |
| | Charlie Waters |

Hayes, recently snubbed for induction into the Pro Football Hall of Fame.

These were also the best of times for the team. Its 7–3 record looked playoff-bound. The Cowboys had never failed to qualify for postseason from that height. But when its offensive line floundered, this one finished 9–7 and out of the money.

Two games frittered away late were the haunting difference. Washington scored on two long passes in the final four minutes to win 14–13. Seattle won 13–10 at the final gun on a 50-yard field goal set up by an interception. Parcells had those games in mind in a season recap.

"If a couple of things had gone our way we could have been sitting here with 14 wins, and at the same time if a couple of things had gone the other way we probably could have 10 losses," he said. "I definitely think our team is used to playing in tight quarters, which is something I like about the team. If you can ever get that characteristic under your belt, that can serve you very, very well."

Yet all was not glum in retrospect. Of the NFC tournament semifinalists, the Cowboys beat Carolina 24–20 and had Seattle whipped for 58 minutes, both on the road. They also dominated AFC West champion Denver before losing 24–21. A background of playing elite teams to the wire appeared the underlying message from Parcells.

The year 2006 dawned in splendor for the franchise. Troy Aikman and Wright were elected to the Pro Football Hall of Fame. Aikman was a first-year eligible choice; Wright was a candidate of the Senior Committee that recommends worthy players long overlooked. The only downer note was the exclusion of Michael Irvin for the second consecutive year.

"My 13-year career in the NFL paralleled that of Rayfield and Ron Yary [Minnesota], and during that time the three of us were always battling for Pro Bowl tackle spots in the NFC and recognition of being in the elite class at the position," said Dan Dierdorf, Hall of Fame lineman of the St. Louis Cardinals. "I've always felt that it wasn't fair that Ron and I were inducted before Rayfield, and that his selection is long overdue."

Cowboy fullback Daryl Johnston's tribute to Aikman spoke to the competitive definition of his quarterback. "Troy was solely motivated by winning championships," said Johnston. "With his ego, he was able to put aside the fact that he didn't have numbers like John Elway, Dan Marino, or

Joe Montana, but that was not what his personality was about. He was about winning championships."

Thus the Cowboys membership in the Hall of Fame swelled to seven players—the others Bob Lilly, Roger Staubach, Tony Dorsett, Randy White, and Mel Renfro—plus coach Tom Landry and Schramm.

Meanwhile Parcells agreed to a one-year extension of his contract through 2007. The Cowboys are in much better shape than when he arrived. His history of building deep playoff contenders suggests the Cowboys will be even better by the time Parcells is through.

With this end in mind, Jones made two shocking moves in March. He signed receiver Terrell Owens to a three-year, $25 million contract that rocked the NFL and fractured his fan base into pro-con camps. And for the first time he invested heavily—$5 million over three years—in a proven kicker, Mike Vanderjagt of Indianapolis.

The Owens deal made tsunami-sized waves, based on his history as a mega-talent who created turmoil in San Francisco and Philadelphia by criticizing quarterbacks Jeff Garcia and Donovan McNabb. He'd also become captain of the local All-Villain Team in 2000 by staging a post-touchdown preen on the midfield star at Texas Stadium until George Teague bounced him aside.

"This is America's Team," said Owens upon arrival. "I feel right at home. I'm a star among stars now."

Salary cap–related aftershocks produced prominent casualties: future Hall of Fame guard Larry Allen, Keyshawn Johnson, La'Roi Glover, and Dan Campbell. Injuries retired Dat Nguyen, and play-caller Sean Payton left to become head coach of the New Orleans Saints, leaving Parcells the heir-apparent for that duty.

The schedule offers the Cowboys few favors. Six of their first nine games are away. Worse, three consecutive road games at Carolina, Washington, and Arizona loom at midseason. Research reveals that 92 teams since 1990 have played three in a row away and only 32 survived to make the playoffs.

The presence of Owens overshadowed all these factors. His forecast for the 2006 season: "Get your popcorn ready," he advised. "It's gonna be a show."

# ANSWERS TO
# TRIVIA QUESTIONS

**Page 3:** Kicker Allen Green scored the winning points when the Cowboys won their first NFL game.

**Page 5:** Receiver Mike Renfro was a ball boy of the '60s who later played for the Cowboys.

**Page 9:** The Cowboys held their first training camp in Forest Grove, Oregon.

**Page 12:** In the early '60s, Eddie LeBaron made that comment.

**Page 15:** Sid Gillman was considered for the Cowboys' first head coach position.

**Page 16:** Running back Walt Garrison.

**Page 29:** Dan Reeves was the first Cowboy to score eight touchdowns both rushing and receiving. He pulled off the trick in 1966.

**Page 34:** Rayfield Wright, who joined the Cowboys in 1967.

**Page 40:** Craig Morton's real first name was Larry.

**Page 42:** Center Dave Manders.

**Page 47:** Guard Herb Scott caught the last pass of Roger Staubach's career.

**Page 49:** "If you needed four yards you'd give the ball to Walt and he'd get you four yards. If you needed 20 yards you'd give the ball to Walt and he'd get you four yards."

**Page 50:** Linebacker D.D. Lewis holds the Cowboys record for most appearances in playoff games.

**Page 54:** Burnett Field.

**Page 62:** Cornell Green holds the career club record for most blocked extra points, field goals, and punts. He made 10 (eight fields goals, two extra points).

**Page 64:** Charlie Waters.

**Page 70:** Linebacker Lee Roy Jordan.

**Page 72:** Defensive lineman Pat Toomay.

**Page 82:** Tony Dorsett holds the Cowboys' record for most yards per carry in a career, with 4.4 years per carry.

**Page 86:** Cornerback Cornell Green.

**Page 93:** Ed Jones's first two boxing opponents were Abdullah Muhammad and Yaqui Meneses.

**Page 95:** Placekicker Rafael Septien is the only non back or wide receiver to be among the top five in all-time Cowboys scoring. His 874 points puts him second on the list, behind only Emmitt Smith.

**Page 101:** Mel Renfro.

**Page 108:** Mike Ditka was the first Cowboys assistant coach to win a Super Bowl as head coach of another team. He won with the Chicago Bears in 1985.

**Page 116:** Tom Landry was a defensive back and punter for the New York Giants and the New York Yankees of the AAFC.

**Page 122:** Former bad boy Thomas "Hollywood" Henderson, clean and sober for the past 23 years, won the Texas Lottery.

**Page 126:** Jerry Jones.

**Page 129:** Troy Aikman threw the longest non-scoring pass in club history to Alvin Harper, 90 yards versus San Francisco in 1994.

**Page 133:** Michael Irvin.

**Page 135:** Buffalo held the Cowboys to 10 points in a 13–10 win over the Cowboys.

**Page 137:** Jimmy Johnson's record as head coach of the Cowboys was 51–37.

**Page 141:** Emmitt Smith broke his own record of 1,713 when he rushed for a team record of 1,773 yards in 1995.

**Page 146:** Kevin Williams.

**Page 152:** Defensive End Greg Ellis holds the Cowboys record for the longest return of a fumble, 98 yards against Arizona in 1999.

**Page 151:** Emmitt Smith, Michael Irvin, and Troy Aikman were the "Triplets." Aikman said the moniker "implied that our contributions to the Cowboys were intertwined. It's hard to imagine any one of us enjoying anywhere near the success we had, going it alone. The nickname may have sprung from our on-field achievements but I always thought of it in terms of our personal relationships."

**Page 159:** Bill Parcells once coached at Texas Tech.

# Dallas Cowboys All-Time Roster (through 2005)

Players on this roster have appeared in at least one regular-season or playoff game with the Cowboys.

## A

| | | |
|---|---|---|
| Abram, Dashawn(CB), Wyoming | 2002 | |
| Abrams, Bobby (LB), Michigan | 1992–93 | |
| Adams, David (RB), Arizona | 1987 | |
| Adams, Flozell (T), Michigan State | 1998–2005 | |
| Adams, Keith (LB), Clemson | 2001–02 | |
| Adams. Vashone (DB), Eastern Michigan | 1999 | |
| Adderley, Herb (CB), Michigan State | 1970–72 | |
| Adkins, Margene (WR), Henderson J.C. | 1970–71 | |
| Agee, Tommie (FB), Auburn | 1990–94 | |
| Aikman, Troy (QB), UCLA | 1989–2000 | |
| Akins, Chris (S), Arkansas-Pine Bluff | 1999–2000 | |
| Albritton, Vince (S, LB), Washington | 1984–91 | |
| Alexander, Bubba (LB),Louisiana State | 2001 | |
| Alexander, Ray (WR), Florida A&M | 1988–89 | |
| Alford, Darnell (T), Boston College | 2002 | |
| Allen, Gary (RB), Hawaii | 1983–84 | |
| Allen, Larry (G), Sonoma State | 1994–2005 | |
| Alston, Charles (DE), Bowie State | 2003 | |
| Alworth, Lance (WR), Arkansas | 1971–72 | |
| Anderson, Antonio (DE), Syracuse | 1997–98 | |
| Anderson, Morris (WR), Baylor | 2000 | |
| Anderson, Richie (RB), Penn State | 2003–05 | |

Andrie, George (DE), Marquette — 1962–72
Ankrom, Scott (WR), Texas Christian — 1989
Armstrong, Jimmy (CB), Appalachian State — 1987
Armstrong, Tyji (TE), Mississippi — 1996, 2000
Arneson, Jim (C, G), Arizona — 1973–74
Asher, Bob (T), Vanderbilt — 1970
Atkins, Corey (LB), South Carolina — 2000
Aughtman, Dowe (OL), Auburn — 1984
Avery, John (RB), Mississippi — 2001
Awalt, Rob (TE), San Diego State — 1990–91

## B

| | | |
|---|---|---|
| Babb, Gene (LB, RB), Austin College | 1960–61 | |
| Babinecz, John (LB), Villanova | 1972–73 | |
| Bailey, Robert (CB), Miami (Florida) | 1995 | |
| Baker, Jesse (DE), Jacksonville State | 1986 | |
| Baker, Sam (P, K), Oregon State | 1962–63 | |
| Baldinger, Brian (OL), Duke | 1982–84, 1986–87 | |
| Banks, Gordon (WR), Stanford | 1985–87 | |
| Banks, Tony (QB), Michigan State | 2001 | |
| Barber, Marion (RB), Minnesota | 2005 | |
| Barksdale, Rod (WR), Arizona | 1987 | |
| Barnes, Benny (DB), Stanford | 1972–82 | |
| Barnes, Darian (RB), Hampton | 2004–05 | |
| Barnes, Gary (WR), Clemson | 1963 | |

| | | |
|---|---|---|
| Barnes, Rashidi (S), Colorado | 2002 | |
| Barnes, Reggie (LB), Oklahoma | 1995 | |
| Barnes, Rodrigo (LB), Rice | 1973–74 | |
| Barrow, Michael (LB), Miami | 2005 | |
| Bateman, Marv (P), Utah | 1972–74 | |
| Bates, Bill (S), Tennessee | 1983–97 | |
| Bates, Justin (G), Colorado | 2003 | |
| Bates, Michael (WR), Arizona | 2003 | |
| Batiste, Michael (DT, G), Tulane | 1995 | |
| Baynham, Craig (RB), Georgia Tech | 1968–69 | |
| Beldon, Bob (QB), Notre Dame | 1969–70 | |
| Bell, Jason (CB), UCLA | 2001–02 | |
| Benson, Darren (DT), Trinity Valley | | |
| C.C. (Texas) | 1996–98 | |
| Bercich, Bob (S), Michigan State | 1960–61 | |
| Beriault, Justin (S), Ball State | 2005 | |
| Bethea, Larry (DL), Michigan State | 1978–83 | |
| Beuerlein, Steve (QB), Notre Dame | 1991–92 | |
| Bickerstaff, Erik (FB), Wisconsin | 2003–05 | |
| Bielski, Dick (TE), Maryland | 1960–61 | |
| Bishop, Don (CB), CCLA | 1960–65 | |
| Bjornson, Eric (TE), Washington | 1996–99 | |
| Black, Michael (RB), Washington State | 2000 | |
| Blackwell, Alois (RB), Houston | 1978–79 | |
| Blackwell, Kelly (TE), Texas Christian | 1993 | |
| Blade, Willie (DT), Mississippi State | 2001–05 | |
| Blake, Ricky (RB), Alabama | 1991 | |
| Bledsoe, Drew (QB), Washington State | 2005 | |
| Blount, Alvin (RB), Maryland | 1987 | |
| Boeke, Jim (T), Heidelberg | 1964–67 | |
| Boniol, Chris (K), Louisiana Tech | 1994–96 | |
| Boone, Aaron (WR), Kentucky | 2003 | |
| Bordano, Chris (LB), Southern Methodist | 2000 | |
| Borden, Nate (DE), Indiana | 1960–61 | |
| Borresen, Rich (TE), Northwestern | 1987 | |
| Bowden, Joe (LB), Oklahoma | 2000–01 | |

| | |
|---|---|
| Braatz, Tom (LB), Marquette | 1960 |
| Bradfute, Byron (T), Southern Mississippi | 1960–61 |
| Brady, Kerry (K), Hawaii | 1987 |
| Brady, Rickey (TE), Oklahoma | 2000–01 |
| Brazzell, Chris (WR), Angelo State | 1999–2001 |
| Breunig, Bob (LB), Arizona State | 1975–84 |
| Brice, Alundis (CB), Mississippi | 1995–96 |
| Briggs, Greg (S), Texas Southern | 1995 |
| Brinkley, Lester (DL), Mississippi | 1990 |
| Brinson, Larry (RB), Florida | 1977–79 |
| Brock, Clyde (DT), Utah State | 1962–63 |
| Brooks, Ethan (OT), Williams College | 2005 |
| Brooks, Jamal (LB), Hampton | 2001–04 |
| Brooks, Jermaine (DT), Arkansas | 2003–05 |
| Brooks, Kevin (DT), Michigan | 1985–88 |
| Brooks, Macey (WR), James Madison | 1997 |
| Brooks, Michael (S), North Carolina State | 1990 |
| Brotzki, Bob (T), Syracuse | 1988 |
| Broughton, Willie (DT), Miami (Florida) | 1989–90 |
| Brown, Eric (DB), Savannah State | 1989 |
| Brown, Guy (LB), Houston | 1977–82 |
| Brown, Larry (CB), Texas Christian | 1991–95, 1998 |
| Brown, Otto (DB), Prairie View | 1969 |
| Brownlow, Darrick (LB), Illinois | 1991, 1994 |
| Bryant, Antonio (WR), Pittsburgh | 2002–04 |
| Bryant, Darius (DT), North Carolina State | 2002 |
| Bryant, Matt (K), Baylor | 2004 |
| Brymer, Chris (OL), Southern | |
| California | 1999–2000 |
| Bua, Tony (S), Arkansas | 2005 |
| Bullocks, Amos (RB), Southern Illinois | 1962–64 |
| Burbage, Cornell (WR), Kentucky | 1987–89 |
| Burkett, Jackie (LB), Auburn | 1968–69 |
| Burley, Siaha (WR), Central Florida | 2001 |
| Burnett, Kevin (LB), Tennessee | 2005 |
| Burnette, Dave (T), Central Arkansas | 1987 |

Burton, Ron (LB), North Carolina — 1987–89

Butler, Bill (S), Southern Tennessee/
    Chattanooga — 1960

**C**

Caffey, Lee Roy (LB), Texas A&M — 1971

Campbell, Dan (TE), Texas A&M — 2003–05

Campbell, Khary (LB), Bowling Green — 2002

Campos, Alan (LB), Louisville — 1996

Cannon, Billy (LB), Texas A&M — 1984

Cantrell, Barry (P), Fordham — 2000

Canty, Chris (DE), Virginia — 2005

Capone, Warren (LB), Louisiana State — 1975

Carano, Glenn (QB), Nevada-Las Vegas — 1977–83

Cargile, Steve (S), Columbia — 2004–05

Carmichael, Harold (WR), Southern — 1984

Carrell, Duane (P), Florida State — 1974

Carson, Leonardo (DT), Auburn — 2003–05

Carter, Jamie (DT), Alabama — 2001

Carter, Jon (DT), Pittsburgh — 1989

Carter, Quincy (QB), Georgia — 2001–04

Carthon, Ran (RB), Florida — 2004

Carver, Shante (DE), Arizona State — 1994–97

Case, Scott (S), Oklahoma — 1995

Casillas, Tony (DT), Oklahoma — 1991–93, 1996

Cason, Aveion (RB), Illinois State — 2003–04

Caver, Quinton (LB), Arkansas — 2005

Cerqua, Marq (LB), Carson-Newman — 2001–02, 2005

Cesario, Sal (G), Cal Poly SLO — 1987

Chancey, Robert (RB), No College — 1999

Chandler, Thornton (TE), Alabama — 1986–89

Cheek, Louis (OL), Texas A&M — 1990

Cherry, J'Juan (S), Arizona State — 2001

Chevrier, Randy (DT), McGill College
    (Ontario) — 2001

Chiaverini, Darrin (WR), Colorado — 2001–02

Childress, Ray (DT), Texas A&M — 1996

Chukwuma, Chrys (RB), Arkansas — 2000

Cisowski, Steve (T), Santa Clara — 1987

Clack, Darryl (RB), Arizona State — 1986–89

Clark, Mike (K), Texas A&M — 1968–71, 1973

Clark, Monte (T), Southern California — 1962

Clark, Phil (DB), Northwestern — 1968–69

Clarke, Frank (TE, WR), Colorado — 1960–67

Clay, Hayward (TE), Texas A&M — 1998–99

Claybrooks, DeVone (DT), East Carolina — 2004

Clemens, Sam (QB), Western Illinois — 2002

Clinkscale, Dextor (S), South Carolina State — 1980, 1982–85

Coady, Rich (FS), Texas A&M — 2005

Coakley, Dexter (LB), Appalachian State — 1997–2005

Cobb, Garry (LB), Southern California — 1988–89

Cole, Larry (C), Hawaii — 1968–80

Coleman, Anthony (DB), Baylor — 1987

Coleman, Kenyon (DE), UCLA — 2003–05

Coleman, Lincoln (RB), Baylor — 1993–94

Coleman, Ralph (LB), North Carolina A&T — 1972

Collier, Reggie (QB), Southern Mississippi — 1986

Collins, Dan (G), Boston College — 2001–03

Collins, Javiar (T), Northwestern — 2001–04

Collins, Ryan (TE), St. Thomas, MN — 2001

Colombo, Marc (OT), Boston College — 2005

Colvin, Jim (DT), Houston — 1964–67

Conaty, Bill (C), Virginia Tech — 2003

Condo, John (LB), Maryland — 2005

Cone, Drew (WR), Southern Arkansas — 2000

Cone, Fred (K), Clemson — 1960

Connelly, Mike (C), Utah State — 1960–67

Conrad, Bobby Joe (WR), Texas A&M — 1969

Conrad, J.R. (OL), Oklahoma — 2000

Cooper, Chris (DT), Nebraska-Omaha — 2004

**E**

| | |
|---|---|
| Easmon, Ricky (DB), Florida | 1985 |
| East, Ron (DT), Montana State | 1968–70 |
| Eaton, Chad (DT), Washington State | 2004 |
| Edwards, Dave (LB), Auburn | 1963–75 |
| Edwards, Dixon (LB), Michigan State | 1991–95 |
| Edwards, Kelvin (WR), Liberty | 1987–88 |
| Edwards, Mario (CB), Florida State | 2000–03 |
| Eidson, Jim (G, C), Mississippi State | 1976 |
| Ekuban, Ebenezer (DE), North Carolina | 1999–2003 |
| Elam, Onzy (LB), Tennessee State | 1989 |
| Elliott, Lin (K), Texas Tech | 1992–93 |
| Ellis, Greg (DE), North Carolina | 1998–2005 |
| Emanuel, Kevin (DE), Florida State | 2004 |
| Evans, Demetric (DE), Georgia | 2001–03 |
| Everett, Thomas (S), Baylor | 1992–93 |

**F**

| | |
|---|---|
| Falls, Mike (G), Minnesota | 1960–61 |
| Faulk, Trev (LB), Louisiana State | 2002 |
| Fellows, Ron (CB), Missouri | 1981–86 |
| Ferguson, Jason (NT), Georgia | 2005 |
| Fieldings, Anthony (LB), Morningside College | 1995 |
| Fields, Aaron (DE), Troy State | 2000 |
| Filipovic, Filip (P), South Dakota | 2002 |
| Finley, Clint (S), Nebraska | 2005 |
| Fishback, Joe (S), Carson-Newman | 1993–94 |
| Fisher, Ray (T), Eastern Illinois | 1960 |
| Fisher, Stephen (S), North Carolina | 2000 |
| Fitzgerald, John (C), Boston College | 1971–80 |
| Fitzgerald, Markese (CB), Miami | 2003 |
| Flaherty, Harry (LB), Holy Cross | 1987 |
| Flannery, John (G), Syracuse | 1996 |
| Fleming, Cory (WR), Tennessee | 1994–95 |
| Flinn, Ryan (P), Central Florida | 2004 |

| | |
|---|---|
| Flowers, Richmond (S), Tennessee | 1969–71 |
| Flowers, Richmond (WR), Tennessee-Chattanooga | 2001–02 |
| Folkins, Lee (TE), Washington | 1962–64 |
| Folsom, Steve (TE), Utah | 1987–90 |
| Fontenot, Chris (TE), McNeese State | 2000–01 |
| Ford, Bernard (WR), Central Florida | 1989 |
| Fowler, Ryan (LB), Duke | 2004–05 |
| Fowler, Todd (FB), Stephen F. Austin | 1985–88 |
| Francis, Ron (CB), Baylor | 1987–90 |
| Franckhauser, Tom (CB), Purdue | 1960–61 |
| Frank, Bill (T), Colorado | 1964 |
| Frazier, Derrick (CB), Texas A&M | 1996 |
| Frazier, Lance (CB), West Virginia | 2004–05 |
| Frederick, Andy (T), New Mexico | 1977–81 |
| Fricke, Ben (C), Houston | 1999–2002 |
| Frisch, Byron (DE), Brigham Young | 2001–02 |
| Fritsch, Toni (K), Vienna, Austria | 1971–73, 1975 |
| Frost, Ken (DT), Kentucky | 1961–62 |
| Fry, Bob (T), Kentucky | 1960–64 |
| Fugett, Jean (TE), Amherst | 1972–75 |
| Fujita, Scott (LB), California | 2005 |

**G**

| | |
|---|---|
| Gadsden, Oronde (WR), Winston-Salem | 1995 |
| Gaechter, Mike (S), Oregon | 1962–69 |
| Gainer, Derrick (RB), Florida A&M | 1992–93 |
| Galbraith, Scott (TE), Southern California | 1993–94, 1997 |
| Galloway, Joey (WR), Ohio State | 2000–03 |
| Gamble, Jason (G), Clemson | 2001–02 |
| Gant, Kenneth (CB), Albany State | 1990–94 |
| Garmon, Kelvin (G), Baylor | 1999–2002 |
| Garrett, Jason (QB), Princeton | 1993–99 |
| Garrison, Walt (RB), Oklahoma State | 1966–74 |
| Gay, Everett (WR), Texas | 1988 |

Gent, Pete (WR, TE), Michigan State 1964–68

George, Eddie (RB), Ohio State 2004

Gesek, John (G), California
State-Sacramento 1990–93

Gholston, Kendrick (DE), Louisville 2000

Gibbs, Sonny (QB), Texas Christian 1963

Gibson, Aaron (OT), Wisconsin 2001–02

Glenn, Aaron (S), Texas A&M 2005

Glenn, Terry (WR), Ohio State 2003–05

Glover, La'Roi (DT), San Diego State 2002–05

Glymph, Junior (DE), Carson-Newman 2005

Godfrey, Randall (LB), Georgia 1996–99

Gogan, Kevin (T), Washington 1987–93

Gonzaga, John (DE), No College 1960

Gonzalez, Leon (WR), Bethune Cookman 1985

Goodrich, Dwayne (CB), Tennessee 2000–02

Gordon, Maurice (DT), Texas 2002

Gowdy, Cornell (DB), Morgan State 1986

Gowin, Toby (P), North Texas 1997–99, 2003–04

Graham, DeMingo (T), Hofstra 2004

Granger, Charlie (T), Southern 1961

Granger, Norm (RB), Iowa 1984

Grant, Orantes (LB), Georgia 2000–02

Grau, Jeff (TE), UCLA 2002–03

Gray, Jonathan (T), Texas Tech 2000

Green, Alex (CB), Indiana 1987

Green, Allen (P, K), Mississippi 1961

Green, Cornell (DB), Utah State 1962–74

Gregg, Forrest (G, T), Southern
Methodist 1971

Gregory, Bill (DL), Wisconsin 1971–77

Gregory, Glynn (WR, DB), Southern
Methodist 1961–62

Grottkau, Bob (G), Oregon 1961

Gurode, Andre (G), Colorado 2002–05

Guy, Buzz (G), Duke 1960

## H

Hagen, Halvor (C, G), Weber State 1969–70

Haley, Charles (DE), James Madison 1992–96

Hall, Chris (S), East Carolina 1993

Hall, Darran (KR), Colorado State 2000

Hall, Lemanski (LB), Alabama 1999

Hambrick, Darren (LB), South Carolina 1998–2001

Hambrick, Troy (RB), Savannah State 2000–04

Hamel, Dean (DT), Tulsa 1989–90

Hannah, Shane (G), Michigan State 1995

Hansen, Wayne (LB), Texas Wesleyan 1960

Hardy, Darryl (LB), Tennessee 1995

Hardy, Kevin (LB), Illinois 2002

Harper, Alvin (WR), Tennessee 1991–94, 1999

Harper, Dave (LB), Humboldt State 1990

Harper, Roger (S), Ohio State 1996

Harrell, Reggie (WR), TCU 2005

Harris, Cliff (S), Ouachita 1970–79

Harris, Derrick (FB), Miami 2002

Harris, Duriel (WR), New Mexico State 1984

Harris, Jackie (TE), Northeast Louisiana 2000–01

Harris, Jim (S), Oklahoma 1961

Harris, Rod (WR), Texas A&M 1990

Hart, Lawrence (TE), Southern 2000

Hawkes, Michael (LB), Virginia Tech 2003

Hawthorne, Duane (CB), Northern
Illinois 1999–2002

Hayes, Bob (WR), Florida A&M 1965–74

Hayes, Wendell (RB), Humboldt State 1963

Haynes, Tommy (S), Southern California 1987

Hays, Harold (LB), Southern Mississippi 1963–67

Haywood, Ennis (RB), Iowa State 2002

Healy, Don (DT), Maryland 1960–61

Hegamin, George (T), North Carolina State 1994–96

Hegman, Mike (LB), Tennessee State 1976–88

Heinrich, Don (QB), Washington 1960

| | |
|---|---|
| Hellestrae, Dale (T), Southern Methodist | 1990–2000 |
| Hemsley, Nate (LB), Syracuse | 1998–99 |
| Henderson, Thomas (LB), Langston | 1975–79 |
| Hendrickson, Steve (LB), California | 1989 |
| Hendrix, Manny (CB), Utah | 1986–91 |
| Hendrix, Tim (TE), Tennessee | 1985 |
| Hennings, Chad (DE), Air Force | 1988–2000 |
| Henry, Anthony (CB), South Florida | 2005 |
| Henry, Rocky (WR), Utah | 2001 |
| Henson, Drew (QB), Michigan | 2004–05 |
| Herchman, Bill (DE), Texas Tech | 1960–61 |
| Herrera, Efren (K), UCLA | 1974, 1976–77 |
| Herrion, Thomas (OG), Utah | 2004 |
| Hervey, Edward (WR), Southern California | 1995 |
| Higgs, Mark (RB), Kentucky | 1988 |
| Highsmith, Alonzo (RB), Miami (Florida) | 1990–91 |
| Hilbert, Jon (K), Louisville | 2000–01 |
| Hill, Bill (CB), Rutgers | 1987 |
| Hill, Calvin (RB), Yale | 1969–74 |
| Hill, Rod (CB), Kentucky State | 1982–83 |
| Hill, Tony (DE), Tennessee-Chattanooga | 1991–92 |
| Hill, Tony (WR), Stanford | 1977–86 |
| Hilliard, Cedric (DT), Notre Dame | 2004 |
| Hodge, Damon (WR), Alabama State | 2000–01 |
| Hodson, Tommy (QB), Louisiana State | 1994 |
| Hogeboom, Gary (QB), Central Michigan | 1980–85 |
| Holloway, Johnny (CB), Kansas | 1986 |
| Holmes, Clayton (CB), Carson-Newman | 1992–95 |
| Holt, Issiac (CB), Alcorn State | 1989–92 |
| Homan, Dennis (WR), Alabama | 1968–70 |
| Hoopes, Mitch (P), Arizona | 1975 |
| Horton, Ray (S), Washington | 1989–92 |
| Houser, John (C, G), Redlands | 1960–61 |
| Houston, Bill (WR), Jackson State | 1974 |
| Howard, Carl (CB), Rutgers | 1984 |

| | |
|---|---|
| Howard, David (LB), California State-Long Beach | 1989–90 |
| Howard, Percy (WR), Austin Peay | 1975 |
| Howard, Ron (TE), Seattle | 1974–75 |
| Howley, Chuck (LB), West Virginia | 1961–73 |
| Howton, Bill (WR), Rice | 1960–63 |
| Hoyem, Lynn (C, G), California State-Long Beach | 1962–63 |
| Hudson, George (G), New Mexico State | 2000 |
| Huggins, Johnny (TE), Alabama State | 2000–01 |
| Hughes, Randy (S), Oklahoma | 1975–80 |
| Hughes, Tyrone (PR), Nebraska | 1998 |
| Humphrey, Buddy (QB), Baylor | 1961 |
| Hunt, John (G, T), Florida | 1984 |
| Hunter, Monty (S), Salem | 1982 |
| Hunter, Pete (CB), Virginia Union | 2002–05 |
| Hurd, Jeff (LB), Kansas State | 1987 |
| Hurt, Eric (CB), California State-San Jose | 1980 |
| Husmann, Ed (DT), Nebraska | 1960 |
| Hutcherson, Ken (LB), Livingston State | 1974 |
| Hutchinson, Chad (QB), Stanford | 2002–04 |
| Huther, Bruce (LB), New Hampshire | 1977–80, 1983 |
| Hutson, Tony (G), Northeastern State | 1997–2000 |

## I

| | |
|---|---|
| Ifeanyichukwu, Israel (DE), Southern California | 2001 |
| Irvin, Michael (WR), Miami (Florida) | 1988–2000 |
| Isbell, Joe Bob (G), Houston | 1962–65 |
| Ismail, Raghib (WR), Notre Dame | 1999–2000, 2002 |

## J

| | |
|---|---|
| Jackson, Al (G), Louisiana State | 2000–02 |
| Jackson, Keith (DT), Cheyney (Pennsylvania) | 2000 |
| Jackson, Tim (S), Nebraska | 1989 |
| Jackson, Willie (WR), Florida | 1994 |

| | | | |
|---|---|---|---|
| LeBaron, Eddie (QB), Pacific | 1960–63 | Martin, Aaron (WR), Rutgers | 2003 |
| Lee, Darrell (DE), Florida | 2004 | Martin, Harvey (DE), East Texas State | 1973–83 |
| Lee, Rashard (RB), Middle Tennessee | | Martin, Jamar (FB), Ohio State | 2002–04 |
| State | 2003–05 | Martin, Jonathan (S), South Carolina | 2003 |
| Lehr, Matt (C, G), Virginia Tech | 2001–04 | Martin, Kelvin (WR), Boston College | 1987–92, |
| Lester, Tim (FB), Eastern Kentucky | 1999 | | 1996 |
| Lett, Leon (DE), Emporia State | 1991–2000 | Maryland, Russell (DT), Miami (Florida) | 1991–95, |
| Lewis, D. D. (LB), Mississippi State | 1968, 1970–81 | | 2002 |
| Lewis, Woodley (WR), Oregon | 1960 | Mathis, Kevin (DB), East Texas State | 1997–99 |
| Lies, Michael (G), Kansas | 2000 | Matthews, Ray (WR), Clemson | 1960 |
| Lilja, George (C), Michigan | 1987 | McBriar, Mat (P), Hawaii | 2004–05 |
| Lilly, Bob (DT), Texas Christian | 1961–74 | McCauley, Tango (G), Alabama State | 2004 |
| Lilly, Kevin (DT), Tulsa | 1989 | McCormack, Hurvin (DT), Indiana | 1994–98 |
| Lindell, Rian (K), Washington State | 2000 | McCreary, Bob (T), Wake Forest | 1961 |
| Liscio, Tony (T), Tulsa | 1963–64, | McDaniels, David (WR), Mississippi Valley | 1968 |
| | 1966–71 | McDonald, Paul (QB), Southern California | 1986–87 |
| Livingston, Bruce (DB), Arkansas | 1987 | McDonald, Tommy (WR), Oklahoma | 1964 |
| Livingston, Warren (CB), Arizona | 1961–67 | McFadden, Marques (OL), Arizona | 2002–03 |
| Lockett, J. W. (RB), Central Oklahoma | 1961–62 | McGarity, Wane (WR), Texas | 1999–2001 |
| Lockhart, Eugene (LB), Houston | 1984–90 | McGee, Don (CB), North Texas | 2003 |
| Logan, Obert (S), Trinity Texas | 1965–67 | McGee, Tony (TE), Michigan | 2002–03 |
| Long, Bob (LB), UCLA | 1962 | McIlhenny, Don (RB), Southern Methodist | 1960–61 |
| Longley, Clint (QB), Abeline Christian | 1974–75 | McIntosh, Toddrick (DT), Florida State | 1994 |
| Lothridge, Billy (P, QB), Georgia Tech | 1964 | McIver, Everett (G), Elizabeth City State | 1998–99 |
| Lucas, Anthony (WR), Arkansas | 2001–02 | McKenzie, Damonte (DT), Clemson | 2001 |
| Lucky, Michael (TE), Arizona | 1999–2002 | McKie, Jason (FB), Temple | 2003 |
| Lusk, Gary (WR), Texas A&M-Kingsville | 2003 | McKinney, Jeremy (G), Iowa | 2002 |
| Luttrell, Chad (WR), Henderson State | 2001 | McKinnon, Dennis (WR), Florida State | 1990 |
| | | McKnight, James (WR), Liberty | 1999–2000 |
| **M** | | McLean, Scott (LB), Florida State | 1983 |
| Mackey, Louis (LB), Akron | 2001–03 | McNeil, Ryan (CB), Miami | 2000 |
| Manders, Dave (C), Michigan State | 1964–74 | McSwain, Chuck (RB), Clemson | 1983–84 |
| Manning, Wade (CB), Ohio State | 1979 | Memmelaar, Dale (G), Wyoming | 1962–63 |
| Manns, Denvis (RB), New Mexico State | 1999–2001 | Meredith, Don (QB), Southern Methodist | 1960–68 |
| Marion, Brock (S), Nevada-Reno | 1993–97 | Merritt, Ahmad (WR), Wisconsin | 2005 |
| Marsh, Amos (RB), Oregon State | 1961–64 | Meyers, John (DT), Washington | 1962–63 |

| | | |
|---|---|---|
| Palmer, Mitch (LB), Colorado State | 2002 | |
| Palmer, Paul (RB), Temple | 1989 | |
| Parks, Billy (WR), California State-Long Beach | 1972 | |
| Parmer, Jason (LB), James Madison | 2001 | |
| Parrish, James (T), Temple | 1993–94 | |
| Patera, Jack (LB), Oregon | 1960–61 | |
| Patterson, Elvis (CB), Kansas | 1993 | |
| Pearson, Drew (WR), Tulsa | 1973–83 | |
| Pearson, Preston (RB), Illinois | 1975–80 | |
| Peete, Rodney (QB), Southern California | 1994 | |
| Pelluer, Steve (QB), Washington | 1984–88 | |
| Penn, Jesse (LB), Virginia Tech | 1985–87 | |
| Peoples, George (RB), Auburn | 1982 | |
| Perkins, Don (RB), New Mexico | 1961–68 | |
| Perkins, Ray (DE), Virginia | 1987 | |
| Perryman, Robert (FB), Michigan | 1990 | |
| Peterman, Stephen (G), LSU | 2004–05 | |
| Petersen, Kurt (G), Missouri | 1980–85 | |
| Peterson, Calvin (LB), UCLA | 1974–75 | |
| Petitti, Rob (OT), Pittsburgh | 2005 | |
| Phillips, Kirk (WR), Tulsa | 1984 | |
| Phipps, Joe (LB), Texas Christian | 1999–2000 | |
| Pickens, Carl (WR), Tennessee | 2000 | |
| Pierce, Brett (TE), Stanford | 2004–05 | |
| Pile, Willie (S), Virginia Tech | 2005 | |
| Pinder, Cyril (RB), Illinois | 1973 | |
| Pittman, Kavika (DE), McNeese State | 1996–99 | |
| Pitts, Otis (DT), Louisiana Tech | 2000 | |
| Ploeger, Kurt (DL), Gustavus Adolphus | 1986 | |
| Poimboeuf, Lance (K), Southwest Louisiana | 1963 | |
| Polite, Lousaka (FB), Pittsburgh | 2004–05 | |
| Ponder, David (DT), Florida State | 1985 | |
| Porterfield, Garry (DE), Tulsa | 1965 | |
| Powe, Karl (WR), Alabama State | 1985–86 | |
| Powell, Jemeel (CB), California | 2003–04 | |

| | |
|---|---|
| Pozderac, Phil (T), Notre Dame | 1982–87 |
| Price, Jim (TE), Stanford | 1993 |
| Price, Marcus (OT), LSU | 2005 |
| Price, Peerless (WR), Tennessee | 2005 |
| Procter, Cory (G), Montana | 2005 |
| Pruitt, Mickey (LB), Colorado | 1991–92 |
| Pugh, Jethro (DT), Elizabeth City State | 1965–78 |
| Puleri, Charles (QB), New Mexico State | 2000 |
| Putnam, Duane (G), Pacific | 1960 |

**Q**

| | |
|---|---|
| Quinn, Mike (QB), Stephen F. Austin | 1998–99 |

**R**

| | |
|---|---|
| Rafferty, Tom (G, C), Penn State | 1976–89 |
| Rambo, Key-Yon (WR), Ohio State | 2001–03 |
| Randall, Tom (G), Iowa State | 1978 |
| Randle, Sonny (WR), Virginia | 1968 |
| Ranek, Josh (RB), South Dakota State | 2002 |
| Ratliff, Jeremiah (DT), Auburn | 2005 |
| Rector, Jamaica (WR), Northwest Missouri State | 2005 |
| Reece, Beasley (CB, WR), North Texas | 1976 |
| Reese, Guy (DT), Southern Methodist | 1962–63 |
| Reese, Izell (S), Alabama-Birmingham | 1998, 2000–01, 2005 |
| Reeves, Dan (RB, QB), South Carolina | 1965–72 |
| Reeves, Jacques (CB), Purdue | 2004–05 |
| Renfro, Mel (DB, RB), Oregon | 1964–77 |
| Renfro, Mike (WR), Texas Christian | 1984–87 |
| Rentzel, Lance (WR), Oklahoma | 1968–70 |
| Reynolds, Jerry (T), Nevada-Las Vegas | 1994 |
| Rhome, Jerry (QB), Tulsa | 1965–68 |
| Richards, Curvin (RB), Pittsburgh | 1991–92 |
| Richards, Golden (WR), Hawaii | 1973–78 |
| Richards, Howard (G, T), Missouri | 1981–86 |

| | | |
|---|---|---|
| Richardson, Gloster (WR), Jackson State | 1971 | |
| Ricks, Mikhael (TE), Stephen F. Austin | 2004 | |
| Ridgeway, Colin (K, P), Lamar Tech | 1965 | |
| Ridlon, Jim (S), Syracuse | 1963–64 | |
| Riley, Earl (S), Washington State | 2000–01 | |
| Rivera, Marco (G), Penn State | 2005 | |
| Roach, John (QB), Southern Methodist | 1964 | |
| Roberts, Alfredo (TE), Miami (Florida) | 1991–92 | |
| Robinson, Jeff (TE), Idaho | 2002–05 | |
| Robinson, Larry (RB), Tennessee | 1973 | |
| Robinson, Ray (RB), No College | 2002 | |
| Roche, Brian (TE), San Jose State | 2000 | |
| Roe, Bill (LB), Colorado | 1980 | |
| Rogers, Jacob (T), USC | 2004–05 | |
| Rogers, Phillip (RB), Georgia Tech | 2000 | |
| Rohrer, Jeff (LB), Yale | 1982–87 | |
| Romo, Tony (QB), Eastern Illinois | 2003–05 | |
| Roper, John (LB), Texas A&M | 1993 | |
| Ross, Derek (CB), Ohio State | 2002–03 | |
| Ross, Dominique (RB), Valdosta State | 1995–96 | |
| Rucker, Reggie (WR), Boston College | 1970–71 | |
| Ruffin, Jonathan (K), Cincinnati | 2004 | |
| Russ, Bernard (LB), West Virginia | 2000 | |
| Ruzek, Roger (K), Weber State | 1987–89 | |
| Ryan, Sean (TE), Boston College | 2004–05 | |

**S**

| | | |
|---|---|---|
| Saldi, Jay (TE), South Carolina | 1976–82 | |
| Salonen, Brian (TE, LB), Montana | 1984–85 | |
| Sanchez, Jeff (CB), Tulane | 2003–04 | |
| Sandeman, Bill (DT), Pacific | 1966–67 | |
| Sanders, Darrick (G), Arkansas-Monticello | 2004 | |
| Sanders, Deion (DB), Florida State | 1995–99 | |
| Santiago, O. J. (TE), Kent | 2000 | |
| Sargent, Broderick (FB), Baylor | 1989 | |
| Sawyer, Buzz (P), Baylor | 1987 | |

| | |
|---|---|
| Saxon, Mike (P), San Diego State | 1985–92 |
| Scarlett, Noel (DT), Langston | 2001 |
| Schaum, Greg (DE), Michigan State | 1976 |
| Schoenke, Ray (T), Southern Methodist | 1963–64 |
| Schultz, Chris (T), Arizona | 1983, 1985 |
| Schwantz, Jim (LB), Purdue | 1994–96 |
| Scifres, Steve (G), Wyoming | 1997, 2000 |
| Scott, Chuck (WR), Vanderbilt | 1987 |
| Scott, Darnay (WR), San Diego State | 2002 |
| Scott, Earl (C), Arkansas | 1998–99 |
| Scott, Herb (G), Virginia Union | 1975–84 |
| Scott, Kevin (RB), Stanford | 1989 |
| Scott, Lynn (S), Northwest Oklahoma | 2001–05 |
| Scott, Sean (LB), Maryland | 1988 |
| Scott, Victor (DB), Colorado | 1984–88 |
| Secules, Scott (QB), Virginia | 1988 |
| Seder, Tim (K), Ashland University | 2000–02 |
| Sellers, Ron (WR), Florida State | 1972 |
| Septien, Rafael (K), Southwest Louisiana | 1978–86 |
| Shanle, Scott (LB), Nebraska | 2003–05 |
| Shannon, Randy (LB), Miami (Florida) | 1989–90 |
| Shaw, Bryant (DE), Mississippi State | 2000–01 |
| Shaw, Robert (C), Tennessee | 1979–81 |
| Shearin, Joe (C), Texas | 1987 |
| Shepard, Derrick (WR), Oklahoma | 1989–91 |
| Sherer, Dave (P), Southern Methodist | 1960 |
| Sherrard, Mike (WR), UCLA | 1986 |
| Sherrod, Rick (S), West Virginia | 2003 |
| Shields, Jon (G), Portland State | 1987 |
| Shiver, Clay (C), Florida State | 1996–98 |
| Shy, Les (RB), California State-Long Beach | 1966–69 |
| Simmons, Cleo (TE), Jackson State | 1983 |
| Simmons, Dave (LB), Georgia Tech | 1968 |
| Simmons, Victor (LB), Central State (Ohio) | 1987 |
| Singleton, Al (LB), Temple | 2003–05 |
| Slaten, Joe (T), Southern Methodist | 2002 |

| | | |
|---|---|---|
| Slaton, Tony (G), Southern California | 1990 |
| Slaughter, Chad (T), Alcorn State | 2000–01 |
| Slowinowski, Bob (TE), Virginia Tech | 2002 |
| Smagala, Stan (DB), Notre Dame | 1990–91 |
| Smerek, Don (DL), Nevada-Reno | 1981–87 |
| Smith, Artie (DT), Louisiana Tech | 1998 |
| Smith, Chris (TE), Texas | 2000 |
| Smith, Darrin (LB), Miami (Florida) | 1993–96 |
| Smith, Daryle (T), Tennessee | 1987–88 |
| Smith, Donald (S), Liberty | 1991 |
| Smith, Emmitt (RB), Florida | 1990–2002, |
| | 2005 |
| Smith, J. D. (RB), North Carolina A&T | 1965–67 |
| Smith, Jackie (TE), Northwest Louisiana | 1978 |
| Smith, Jim Ray (G, T), Baylor | 1963–64 |
| Smith, Jimmy (WR), Jackson State | 1992 |
| Smith, Kevin (CB), Texas A&M | 1992–2000 |
| Smith, Myron (LB), Louisiana Tech | 1998 |
| Smith, Sean (DT), Grambling | 1989 |
| Smith, Shaun (DT), South Carolina | 2003–04 |
| Smith, Tarik (RB), California | 1998–99 |
| Smith, Timmy (RB), Texas Tech | 1990 |
| Smith, Tody (DL), Southern California | 1971–72 |
| Smith, Vinson (LB), East Carolina | 1990–92, 1997 |
| Smith, Waddell (WR), Kansas | 1984 |
| Smith, Zuriel (WR), Hampton | 2003–05 |
| Snell, Shannon (G), Florida | 2005 |
| Snyder, Loren (QB), Northern Colorado | 1987 |
| Solomon, Jesse (LB), Florida State | 1989–90 |
| Solomon, Roland (S), Utah | 1980 |
| Solwold, Mike (TE), Wisconsin | 2001 |
| Sparks, Phillippi (CB), Arizona State | 2000 |
| Spears, Marcus (DE), LSU | 2005 |
| Spellman, Alonzo (DE), Ohio State | 1999–2000 |
| Spivey, Sebron (WR), Southern Illinois | 1987 |
| Spotwood, Quinton (WR), Syracuse | 2000 |

| | | |
|---|---|---|
| Spradlin, Danny (LB), Tennessee | 1981–82 |
| Springs, Ron (RB), Ohio State | 1979–84 |
| Stalls, Dave (DE), Northern Colorado | 1977–79 |
| Staubach, Roger (QB), Navy | 1969–79 |
| Steele, Markus (LB), USC | 2001–04 |
| Steele, Robert (WR), Northern Alabama | 1978 |
| Stephens, Larry (DE), Texas | 1963–67 |
| Stepnoski, Mark (C, G), Pittsburgh | 1989–94, |
| | 1999–2001 |
| Stewart, Curtis (RB), Auburn | 1989 |
| Stewart, Daleroy (DT), Southern Mississippi | 2001–04 |
| Stiger, Jim (RB), Washington | 1963–65 |
| Stiggers, Marcus (WR), Colorado | 2001 |
| Still, Bryan (WR), Virginia Tech | 1999 |
| Stincic, Tom (LB), Michigan | 1969–71 |
| Stoerner, Clint (QB), Arkansas | 2000–03 |
| Stone, Ron (T), Boston College | 1993–95 |
| Stoudt, Cliff (QB), Youngstown State | 1990–91 |
| Stoutmire, Omar (DB), Fresno State | 1997–98 |
| Stowe, Otto (WR), Iowa State | 1973 |
| Strayhorn, Les (RB), East Carolina | 1973–74 |
| Strickland, Fred (LB), Purdue | 1996–98 |
| Stubbs, Daniel (DE), Miami (Florida) | 1990–91 |
| Studstill, Darren (S), West Virginia | 1994 |
| Sturgis, Oscar (DE), North Carolina | 1995 |
| Stynchula, Andy (DE), Penn State | 1968 |
| Sualua, Nicky (RB), Ohio State | 1997–98 |
| Suisham, Shaun (K), Bowling Green | 2005 |
| Sullivan, Mike (T), Miami (Florida) | 1991 |
| Swan, Russ (LB), Virginia | 1987 |
| Swartz, Noah (G, T), Toledo | 2003 |
| Sweeney, Kevin (QB), California State-Fresno | 1987–88 |
| Swinton, Reggie (WR), Murray State | 2001–03 |
| Szaferski, Maciek (P), St. Francis (Indiana) | 2002 |

## T

| | | |
|---|---|---|
| Talbert, Don (DE, OT), Texas | 1962, 1965, 1971 |
| Tarullo, Matt (OG), Syracuse | 2005 |
| Tarver, Hurley (CB), Central Oklahoma | 2000 |
| Tautalatasi, Junior (RB), Washington State | 1989 |
| Taylor, Johnathan (DE), Montana State | 2004 |
| Taylor, Tony (RB), Northwestern Louisiana | 2001–02 |
| Teague, George (S), Alabama | 1996, 1998–2001 |
| Tennell, Derek (TE), UCLA | 1992 |
| Tenner, James (G), Alcorn State | 2000 |
| Testaverde, Vinny (QB), Miami | 2004 |
| Thomas, Anthony (RB), Michigan | 2005 |
| Thomas, Bill (RB), Boston College | 1972 |
| Thomas, Blair (RB), Penn State | 1994 |
| Thomas, Broderick (LB), Nebraska | 1996–98 |
| Thomas, Dave (CB), Tennessee | 1993–94 |
| Thomas, Duane (RB), West Texas State | 1970–71 |
| Thomas, Ike (CB), Bishop | 1971 |
| Thomas, Robert (FB), Henderson State | 1998–2002 |
| Thompson, Broderick (G), Kansas | 1985 |
| Thompson, Tyson (RB), San Jose State | 2005 |
| Thornton, Bruce (CB), Georgia | 2004–05 |
| Thornton, Bruce (DL), Illinois | 1979–81 |
| Thornton, Kalen (LB), Texas | 2004–05 |
| Thurman, Dennis (DB), Southern California | 1978–85 |
| Tickles, Marlon (DT), Tulane | 2005 |
| Timmer, Kirk (LB), Montana State | 1987 |
| Tippins, Ken (LB), Middle Tennessee State | 1989 |
| Titensor, Glen (G), Brigham Young | 1981–86, 1988 |
| Tolbert, Brandon (LB), Georgia | 1998–2000 |
| Tolbert, Tony (DE), Texas-El Paso | 1989–97 |
| Tolver, J. R. (WR), San Diego State | 2005 |
| Toomay, Pat (DE), Vanderbilt | 1970–74 |
| Townes, Willie (DE), Tulsa | 1966–68 |
| Tramel, Jasmine (S), Mississippi Valley State | 2000 |

| | |
|---|---|
| Tremble, Greg (S), Georgia | 1995 |
| Truax, Billy (TE), Louisiana State | 1971–73 |
| Trusty, Landon (TE), Central Arkansas | 2004–05 |
| Tubbs, Jerry (LB), Oklahoma | 1960–67 |
| Tucker, B. J. (CB), Wisconsin | 2003 |
| Tucker, Jason (WR), Texas Christian | 1999–2001 |
| Tucker, Ross (G, T), Princeton | 2002–03 |
| Tucker, Torrin (G, T), Southern Mississippi | 2003–05 |
| Tugbenyoh, Mawuko (LB), California | 2001 |
| Tuinei, Mark (OT, DL), Hawaii | 1983–97 |
| Turner, Jimmie (LB), Presbyterian | 1984 |

## U

| | |
|---|---|
| Ulafale, Mike (DT), Brigham Young | 1996–97 |
| Underwood, Dimitrius (DE), Michigan State | 2000–01 |

## V

| | |
|---|---|
| Van Hoy, Chris (DT), Louisiana Tech | 2005 |
| Van Raaphorst, Dick (K), Ohio State | 1964 |
| Vanderbeek, Matt (LB, DE), Michigan State | 1993–94 |
| Veingrad, Alan (OL), East Texas State | 1991–92 |
| Villanueva, Danny (P, K), New Mexico State | 1965–67 |
| Volk, Dave (OL), Nebraska | 2002–04 |
| Vollers, Kurt (G, T), Notre Dame | 2002–05 |

## W

| | |
|---|---|
| Wagstaff, James (OT), North Carolina | 2001 |
| Walen, Mark (DT), UCLA | 1987–88 |
| Walker, Gary (OL), Boston University | 1987 |
| Walker, Herschel (RB), Georgia | 1986–89, 1996–97 |
| Walker, Louis (LB), Colorado State | 1974 |
| Walker, Malcolm (C), Rice | 1966–69 |
| Wallace, Rodney (G, T), New Mexico | 1971–73 |

| | | | | |
|---|---|---|---|---|
| Walls, Everson (CB), Grambling | 1981–89 | Wilbur, John (T), Stanford | 1966–69 |
| Walsh, Steve (QB), Miami (Florida) | 1989–90 | Wiley, Marcellus (DE), Columbia | 2004–05 |
| Walter, Mike (LB), Oregon | 1983 | Wiley, Michael (RB), Ohio State | 2000–03 |
| Walter, Tyson (C, T), Ohio State | 2002–05 | Wilkins, Greg (DT), Langston | 1999-2000 |
| Walton, Bruce (G), UCLA | 1973–75 | Williams, Ben (DT), Minnesota | 2001 |
| Ward, Dedric (WR), Northern Iowa | 2004 | Williams, Charlie (CB), Bowling | |
| Ware, Demarcus (DE), Troy State | 2005 | Green State | 1995–2000 |
| Ware, Derek (TE), Central Oklahoma | 1996 | Williams, Erik (T), Central State (Ohio) | 1991–2000 |
| Warren, Chris (RB), Ferrum | 1998–2000 | Williams, Joe (RB), Wyoming | 1971 |
| Warren, John (P), Tennessee | 1983–84 | Williams, John (FB), Wisconsin | 1985 |
| Washington, James (S), UCLA | 1990–94 | Williams, Kevin (WR), Miami (Florida) | 1993–96 |
| Washington, Mark (CB), Morgan State | 1970–78 | Williams, Lenny (CB), Southern | 2004–05 |
| Waters, Charlie (DB), Clemson | 1970–78, | Williams, Martinez (WR), New Mexico | 2001 |
| | 1980–81 | Williams, Randal (WR), New Hampshire | 2001–05 |
| Watkins, Kendell (TE), Mississippi State | 1995–97 | Williams, Robert (CB), Baylor | 1987–93 |
| Watts, Randy (DE), Catawba | 1987 | Williams, Roy (S), Oklahoma | 2002–05 |
| Wayt, Russell (LB), Rice | 1965 | Williams, Sherman (RB), Alabama | 1995–99 |
| Weatherington, Colston (DE), | | Williams, Stepfret (WR), Northeast | |
| Central Missouri State | 2001–03 | Louisiana | 1996–97 |
| Welch, Claxton (RB), Oregon | 1969–71 | Williams, Tyrone (CB), Nebraska | 2004 |
| Wells, Norm (G), Northwestern | 1980 | Williams, Tyrone (WR), Western Ontario | 1993 |
| Westberry, Gary (C), Hampton | 1987 | Willis, Ken (K), Kentucky | 1990–91 |
| Westbrook, Bryant (CB), Texas | 2002 | Willis, Mitch (DT), Southern Methodist | 1990 |
| Whalen, James (TE), Kentucky | 2000–04 | Wilson, Robert (FB), Texas A&M | 1994 |
| Wheatley, Austin (TE), Iowa | 2001–02 | Wilson, Steve (WR, CB), Howard | 1979–81 |
| Wheaton, Kenny (DB), Oregon | 1997–99 | Wilson, Wade (QB), East Texas State | 1995–97 |
| White, Bob (OL), Rhode Island | 1987–89 | Wingrove, Ryan (DE), Bowling Green | 2004 |
| White, Chris (DE), Southern | 2001 | Wisener, Gary (WR), Baylor | 1960 |
| White, Danny (QB, P), Arizona State | 1976–88 | Witherspoon, Terry (FB), Clemson | 2001 |
| White, Gerald (FB), Michigan | 1987 | Witten, Jason (TE), Tennessee | 2003–05 |
| White, Randy (DT, LB), Maryland | 1975–88 | Woodson, Darren (S), Arizona State | 1992–2004 |
| Whitfield, A. D. (RB), North Texas | 1965 | Woolsey, Rolly (DB), Boise State | 1975 |
| Whittingham, Fred (LB), California | | Wortham, Barron (LB), Texas-El Paso | 2000 |
| Polytechnic-San Luis Obispo | 1969 | Wright, Alexander (WR), Auburn | 1990–92 |
| Widby, Ron (P), Tennessee | 1968–71 | Wright, Anthony (QB), South Carolina | 2000–02 |
| Widell, Dave (T), Boston College | 1988–89 | Wright, Brad (QB), New Mexico | 1982 |